C000186028

Cambridge Five Spy Ring, Part 10 of 42

The Federal Bureau of Investigation (FBI)

The BiblioGov Project is an effort to expand awareness of the public documents and records of the U.S. Government via print publications. In broadening the public understanding of government and its work, an enlightened democracy can grow and prosper. Ranging from historic Congressional Bills to the most recent Budget of the United States Government, the BiblioGov Project spans a wealth of government information. These works are now made available through an environmentally friendly, print-on-demand basis, using only what is necessary to meet the required demands of an interested public. We invite you to learn of the records of the U.S. Government, heightening the knowledge and debate that can lead from such publications.

Included are the following Collections:

Budget of The United States Government
Presidential Documents
United States Code
Education Reports from ERIC
GAO Reports
History of Bills
House Rules and Manual
Public and Private Laws

Code of Federal Regulations
Congressional Documents
Economic Indicators
Federal Register
Government Manuals
House Journal
Privacy act Issuances
Statutes at Large

Mr. Tolson ———
Mr. Boardman ———
Mr. Nichols ———
Mr. Belmont ———
Mr. Harbo ———
Mr. Mohr ———
Mr. Parsons ———
Mr. Rosen ———
Mr. Tamm ———
Mr. Sizoo ———
Mr. Winterrowd ———
Tele. Room ———
Mr. H. Joman ———
Mr. (Gandy) ———

WHY they went WHERE they are

GEOFFREY HOARE

turns the last page of his dossier on
a mystery- that set the world talking

WHY did Donald Maclean disappear? Why did he desert his wife and children, his job —that enviable job in the Foreign Service which held so brilliant a future—and his country, to go over, as it must be presumed he did, to the implacable enemies of his own way of life?

C.B. MacDonald

RE: DONALD DUART MacLEAN, et al
    ESPIONAGE - R
    (Bufile 100-374183)

NEW CHRONICLE
SEPTEMBER 11, 1954
LONDON, ENGLAND

100-374183

NOT RECORDED
191 SEP 29 1954

420

These are not steps a man takes lightly and it is clear that for many months before the final decision Donald Maclean lived in such a terrifying agony of indecision and guilt that his health was affected.

He was of the ill-starred generations who grew to maturity between the two world wars, and whose impressionable years were lived beneath the appalling shadow of Fascism.

Watched ?

In his latter years at Cambridge, in company with many hundreds of other liberal-minded young intellectuals, he became a Communist, because Communism was synonymous with anti-Fascism; to defeat Hitler he rallied to Stalin.

I suggest the Russian Intelligence Service kept a close watch on the careers of many of these former university Communists.

In the middle 'forties the Soviet Union was concerned above all with atomic information, but what might be termed a by-product of our possession of the atomic bomb, our atomic policy, was a high priority. And that made members of the diplomatic service valuable to the Russians and likely to be approached if there was just a hint that they were approachable.

Was Donald Maclean so approached? I do not think anyone knows. It seems impossible from the appointments he held before his flight that the authorities had any suspicions of him.

But there are two inescapable facts.

The first is that he did disappear and official opinion is that he is behind the Iron Curtain. Mr. Selwyn Lloyd, Minister of State for Foreign Affairs, said in reply to a question on January 24, 1954, that "if anyone were to presume that Maclean and Burgess are behind the Iron Curtain, he would probably be right."

The second is the £2,000 Donald sent to Melinda through Mrs. Dunbar. Donald left his home at Tatsfield on May 25, as hard up as ever, and leaving debts behind him: the money was sent by Swiss banks on August 1—an interval of 67 days, from which should be deducted the time it took Donald to get from Tatsfield to wherever he went, and also the time it took for the arrangements to be made to send a messenger to Switzerland to dispatch the money.

Neither need be long, but together they probably cut the actual time in which, in some quite inconceivable conditions, Donald might have earned that sum in addition to whatever it cost him to live, to around 60 days. Was that possible? Is it feasible? Obviously not.

There remain two possibilities: firstly, that he was paid in advance for services to be rendered; secondly, that he was being paid for past services. Which is the more likely?

The combination of these two facts—that Donald deserted to Russia and that in a remarkably short time was in a position not only to send Melinda a large sum of money, but also to obtain permission and assistance from his new masters to do so—points in one direction, and one only: that Donald was approached by Russian agents and did work for them, probably long before he fled.

Exploited

Donald was pitifully vulnerable. He must have appeared an ideal man to be approached by the ruthless agents of a country ready to take advantage of any human weakness or any misplaced idealism.

How much do the British authorities really know of the disappearance of these two men? In his statement to the House of Commons on June 11, 1951, seventeen days after Burgess and Maclean disappeared, Mr. Herbert Morrison said:

"The security aspects of the case are under investigation and it is not in the public interest to disclose them."

That was three years ago, and with practically no variation it has been the line taken by Foreign Office spokesmen ever since.

But with Melinda we enter the realm of pure emotion in which reason plays little part.

When she drove off from Geneva with her three small children on that sultry September afternoon exactly a year ago she was, knowingly and of her own free will, going into exile.

Persuaded

She was going to join a husband who had deserted her, with whom she had been nearly continuously unhappy in their thirteen years of married life, and she was doing this although she had decided to divorce him and try to remake her shattered life. And she was going in the full knowledge of the grievous hurt her action would cause her mother, her family and her friends.

Why did she go?

Obviously Melinda was contacted by agents speaking in Donald's name for several months before she eventually went. They were probably men and women of her own class and either of her or Donald's nationality.

And they were supremely clever. They probably told her Donald was "fighting for peace —helping to build a new and better world." They certainly played on her maternal instincts and gave her a glowing picture of the splendid future the children would have in the Soviet Union.

Donald's excellent position, his fine house, comfortable living conditions would be stressed. None of this would have taken in a woman who had kept herself well-informed on world affairs: but Melinda had been supremely disinterested.

Yet beneath all this there must have been some kind of affection for Donald. The whole thing is meaningless, impossible, unbelievable without that. For Melinda was not logical; she was guided by her emotions—and this final decision must have been taken in emotion and agony. She must have lived in the bottomless pit of hell in the weeks, possibly months, before she finally fled to join her man.

She must have known the sorrow and worry her going would cause her mother: the pitiful thin little letter she was allowed to send showed that.

But against the lingering ashes of her love for Donald, against the sparkling mirage of life to which she was being drawn, none of this mattered. He had called her back to him—and so she went. She was, in a way, justifying herself to the world—and to herself. She was no longer deserted, no longer unwanted; that was a salve to her hurt pride" and a gratification of her love and her desire.

Where are they now, Donald, Melinda and the three children?

I believe from reliable information I have obtained, not from British sources, that Donald is one of the chiefs of the Soviet Government's Psychological Warfare Department. He is living in a sort of satellite city some 60 miles from Moscow which was built solely to house the many various foreigners working for the Russian Government in this particular field.

Guarded

It is a cross between a compound and a prison: the inmates have excellent living conditions, large, comfortable houses and gardens, shops, clubs, schools—but no freedom of movement. There are guards all around, ostensibly to protect the great radio transmitters, but also to see that no one leaves without permission. On the rare occasions any of the foreigners have to go to Moscow or elsewhere in Russia armed guards accompany them.

It is there, in this town with no name, that Melinda and the children joined Donald. She was almost certainly told that if she did not like the life there she would be free to leave, taking her children with her. Will the Soviet keep that promise? It seems highly unlikely.

THE END

[World copyright]

421

THREE LITTLE FACTS—9 centimetres
by 6 centimetres—SHOW THAT...

Melinda

PLANNED

to disappear

THE
MISSING
MACLEANS
14th Instalment

by

GEOFFREY HOARE

NOT RECORDED
141 SEP 21 1954

O.B. MacDonald

JUN 22 1976
PER FOIA REQUEST

100-274183

RE: DONALD DUART MACLEAN, ET AL
    ESPIONAGE - R
    (Bufile 100-374183)

NEWS CHRONICLE
SEPTEMBER 10, 1954
LONDON, ENGLAND

OFFICE OF THE LEGAL ATTACHE

LONDON, E.

422

ON Wednesday night, September 16, last year—five days after Melinda disappeared—I arrived in Geneva from Paris. I saw Mrs. Dunbar the following day when she told me the story as it then appeared to her. Her conclusions, and mine too, were that Melinda had been lured away. We did not think she had actually been kidnapped, but we were certain that she had not gone of her own free will.

Of the complete honesty of Mrs. Dunbar's original story which was also what she had told M.I.5 and the Swiss Police, I have not and had not at the time the slightest doubt: it contained the facts *as she then saw them.*

It was a case of someone being too intimately concerned with events to be able to see them clearly, of daily contact obscuring the all-important small details.

Two shocks

In the account Mrs. Dunbar then gave me, published in the *News Chronicle* on Thursday, September 17, she said: "They had no other clothes and Melinda took only one small suitcase with nightclothes for the children, and one for herself. In that, I believe, she had mainly summer things."

It was five weeks after she had left Geneva that Mrs. Dunbar returned there with her daughters Harriet and Catherine, who, once again, had flown over from America to be by their mother's side, to close up the flat in the Rue des Alpes.

And almost immediately she made two startling discoveries which told her without possibility of doubt that contrary to her earlier impression Melinda had planned her flight in advance—had known when she drove off with the children that she might well never return.

Mrs. Dunbar's first grief-stricken impression that Melinda had taken only things she would normally have needed for a week-end visit was primarily based on what she saw her put into the car.

And she saw Melinda leave the flat with only one suitcase, two large raffia hold-alls which they had brought back from Majorca, and a little red overnight bag provided for their passengers by the big air companies and which contained Melinda's toilet requisites.

The fact that the expensive American suitcase was deceptively roomy and could contain far more than on first sight appeared possible, and that the hold-alls were deep and capacious, did not then strike her. Nor did she realise that Melinda could have packed other things into the car beforehand.

When Mrs. Dunbar had made her original check-up in the closet in the rather dark passage in the flat she had been far too upset to see or think clearly. A quick glance showed her Melinda's mink coat and evening dress. But nothing had been properly tidied away since their return from their long holiday, and hanging in the same closet were dresses of her own.

Then, in the chests of drawers were piles of clothes which she had taken for Melinda's, for it was there that Melinda usually kept her underclothes. Now on closer examination these proved to belong to the children and it required only a short examination for her to discover that Melinda had taken all her clothes with her, everything from suits and dresses down to the new underclothes Mrs. Dunbar had bought for her in New York a few months before, everything except her mink coat and an ex-

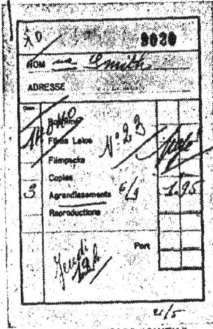

THE NAME READS "SMITH"
This photographer's envelope revealed that Melinda, using the name "Mrs. Smith," ordered—and collected on May 21—three passport size pictures

pensive new evening dress. She had taken almost nothing belonging to the children.

The second discovery was a large sheet of 24 Polyphotos of the three children, with a little envelope with photographer's directions clipped to it.

Mrs. Dunbar was extremely surprised that she knew nothing about these photos and had never seen them before.

Not only would Melinda have told her if she were thinking of having a photograph of the children, but they would eagerly have examined the photographs directly they were obtained from the shop, so Mrs. Dunbar inspected the envelope carefully.

Evidence!

And she saw that Melinda, in the name of "Mrs. Smith," had ordered three enlargements of photograph No. 23—and had called for them on May 21, two days before she, Mrs. Dunbar, arrived back from America, called for them in fact while Mrs. Dunbar was in Paris and in nearly daily telephonic communication with her.

And, Mrs. Dunbar also found the enlargements of the photograph, which itself measured 4.7cms. by 4.5cms., were to be 9cms. by 6cms.—the size required for American passports and those of some of the Iron Curtain countries.

Melinda and the children travelled usually on Melinda's British passport which requires a 7cm. by 5cm. photograph. Both the passport and the enlargements were missing and presumably Melinda had taken them with her.

These two pieces of evidence were entirely conclusive in our opinion: Melinda's disappearance had been planned at least four months before it took place.

[*World copyright*]

The trail Melinda took a year ago this week-end

THE MISSING MACLEANS

Thirteenth Instalment

THE day after Melinda's mother received the telegram from Territet the next clue to the missing family's movements was found.

On September 17, 1953, six days after they disappeared, it set the investigators on a trail which petered out on the borders of the Russian zone of Austria, but which most clearly indicated that Melinda had gone to join her husband.

It was the discovery in a Lausanne garage of her black Chevrolet car. The proprietor told the police it had been left by a woman with three small children not long before 7 p.m. on the previous Friday — six days earlier—and a ticket stuck beneath the windscreen-wiper indicated that it was to be called for the day after its discovery — Friday September 18.

She knew

This proved conclusively that, sometime at least after she left her apartment in Geneva, Melinda knew she would not be returning on the Sunday evening, as she had told her mother. It also showed that she knew then that she was not going to spend the week-end with friends in a villa at Territet. But whether she knew these things before she left home we do not know.

The discovery of the car, only a hundred yards or so from Lausanne station, soon led to the next step. Melinda and her children, it was found, had taken the 6.58 p.m. train from Lausanne to Zurich on that Friday evening.

She was identified by a ticket collector who had been on duty on the train, and also by a Swiss professor who was travelling on it and who noticed a worried-looking Melinda and her three children boarding it at Lausanne.

Evidence soon came to light that Melinda and her family left the train at Zurich. For a day or two there were doubts about her next movement, for she was

RE: DONALD DUART MacLEAN, et al
      ESPIONAGE - R
      (Bufile 100-374183)

NEWS CHRONICLE
SEPTEMBER 9, 1954
LONDON, ENGLAND

C.B. MacDonald 700-374183

4/24

FRIDAY—SEPTEMBER 11th
LEAVES CAR NEAR STATION
BOARDS 6.58 p.m. TRAIN

CHANGES TO
ARLBERG EXPRESS

SATURDAY—SEPTEMBER 12th
LEAVES TRAIN 9 a.m.

SAME DAY—9.30 a.m.
DRIVES AWAY IN
AMERICAN CAR

The lady vanishes— in a BIG CAR

by GEOFFREY HOARE

wrongly identified as having been seen at Vienna station.

What in fact she did was to catch the Arlberg express at Zurich, but to leave it, early Saturday morning, at the small Tyrolean village of Schwarzach St. Veit, 40 miles from Salzburg.

Identification here was provided by an unnamed American colonel who was travelling on the Arlberg to Vienna train. He shared a first-class carriage with the Maclean family, who had not sleepers although it was a night journey.

When he heard of Mrs. Maclean's disappearance he gave information to the American authorities in Vienna, who informed the Swiss Police, who in their turn told the French Police, who passed it on to Mrs. Dunbar.

His description of the pathetic little family who travelled with him that night is far too vivid and accurate to leave any room for doubt. The two fair-haired little boys in grey flannel suits who told him they went to school in Geneva; the one expanding suitcase and the two raffia hold-alls from Majorca; Melinda and her clothes—the bright blue three-quarter length coat—and a detail which is so wholly convincing that nothing else is really needed, the fact that she was wearing a rather cheap little masculine wrist-watch.

In fact, Melinda, having broken the bracelet of her own watch, was using one which Mrs. Dunbar had bought for Fergus, an inexpensive watch of the kind one would normally give to a nine-year-old boy.

The colonel saw them leave the train at Schwarzach St. Veit around 9 on the morning of Saturday, September 12.

Trail ends

If further identification were necessary, it was supplied by a porter at Schwarzach St. Veit station who helped the Macleans off the train, saw them go into the restaurant, and then, about 30 minutes later, drive away in a large American car which had arrived while they were drinking their coffee. The driver was described as a slim man of average height who spoke German with an Austrian accent.

That was the end of the trail. Melinda, like Donald before her, had gone beyond the boundaries over which Western investigation could easily follow her. This fairly rapidly gathered evidence, for the inquiry started on Tuesday, September 15, and was concluded five days later, was considered convincing enough for the Swiss Police to announce that the hunt was off as it was clear that "no purpose would be served by a further search."

There are, however, several points in the actual mechanics of the journey from Geneva to the Austrian frontier which have not been cleared up. In the first place, Melinda left home in her quite fast and powerful car at 3.30 on the Friday afternoon.

The next verified appearance was at the garage in Lausanne just before 7 p.m.—three and a half hours later. The distance between the two points is however only 40 miles—not much more than three-quarters of an hour's drive. What did she do, and where did she go, in the meantime?

She gave herself, or was given, remarkably little time to park the car and conduct her little party, with a certain amount of luggage and a baby in arms, from the garage to the station. Somebody must have helped.

It is clear to me that it was during this time, this unexplained three hours, that Melinda saw whoever it was who was, instructed to contact her, and received her final instructions.

It is almost certain, too, that the tickets for her long journey were given to her before she got to the station, for not only had she, so far as is known, barely enough money, but she certainly had no time to take tickets at Lausanne.

From what Mrs. Dunbar told me I estimated that Melinda left Geneva with around £30 in Swiss francs; and she drew this money from the bank that afternoon at her mother's request.

My colleague Hugh McLeave, one of the News Chronicle crime reporters, who followed the trail from Geneva to Schwarzach St. Veit and who obtained the reliable and detailed identification by the porter at the little Austrian station, worked it out as follows:

One first-class ticket for herself and two halves for the boys from Lausanne to Zurich: £7 18s.

From Zurich to Buchs, on the Austrian frontier, would cost £4 6s. for the three of them, and from Buchs onwards another £8 12s.

Spent out

The total for actual fares was therefore £20 16s., without taking into consideration any additional expenses such as meals, porters, and anything she might have had to spend in Switzerland, after she left her Rue des Alpes flat in Geneva and before she caught the train.

It could be done, but it would have left a very small balance with which to face unknown adventures or any emergency should anything go wrong, as for example, should she suddenly have wished to go back.

[World copyright]

425

| Mr. Tolson |
| Mr. Boardman |
| Mr. Nichols |
| Mr. Belmont |
| Mr. Harbo |
| Mr. Mohr |
| Mr. Parsons |
| Mr. Rosen |
| Mr. Tamm |
| Mr. Sizoo |
| Mr. Winterrowd |
| Tele. Room |
| Mr. Holloman |
| Miss Gandy |

Telegram — from the place nobody thought to watch

THE MISSING MACLEANS

Twelfth Instalment

by GEOFFREY HOARE

DELETED COPY SENT   C.B. Mac Donald
BY LETTER JUN 23 1970
PER FOIA REQUEST

RE: DONALD DUART MacLEAN, et al
ESPIONAGE – R
(Bufile 100-374183)

NEWS CHRONICLE
SEPTEMBER 18, 1954
LONDON, ENGLAND

170 SEP 17 1954

7398

5 5 SEP 20

OFFICE OF THE LEGAL ATTACHE
AMERICAN EMBASSY
LONDON, ENGLAND

426

WHEN Melinda and the children drove off so hurriedly from Geneva on that sunny Friday afternoon a year ago this week it did not for a moment occur to Mrs. Dunbar that she would not see them again in two days' time.

And even when they did not arrive on the Sunday evening she was worried but not seriously alarmed. Alarm came Monday morning, and it was then, on September 14, 1953, that she took steps to inform M.I.5.

Her first attempt to get into touch with the authorities in London was not very successful. The British Consul-General in Geneva, Mr. Lambert, who had been extremely kind to Melinda, had recently left on promotion to the more important post of Consul-General in Paris, and Mrs. Dunbar did not know his successor.

When she telephoned to the British Consulate at 11.40 a.m. she had first to explain who she was—which she did by saying that she was the mother-in-law of Donald Maclean. This seemed to strike no chord, and so she asked if she could speak to the Consul-General on an urgent matter.

She was told she could not see anyone before 2 p.m., as all the senior members of the Consulate had gone to the airport to meet the Lord Mayor of London.

Mrs. Dunbar waited in growing anxiety until after luncheon and then went to the Consulate, which was only a short distance from her apartment.

Reported missing

She saw one of the Consuls and told him that her daughter, Melinda Maclean, a British subject, and her three children were missing, and asked him to inform London immediately.

He said her information would be "sent on to London through the proper channels"—which she rightly took to be the mails.

Mrs. Dunbar replied that before they had all left London M.I.5 had asked her to let them know urgently if anything out of the ordinary happened. This was urgent, she repeated.

The official said: "Now, Mrs. Dunbar, I'm sure your daughter will return soon. But I will pass on your information through the proper channels."

Mrs. Dunbar returned to her apartment in despair. For the fiftieth time she went through her papers but could not find the telephone number she wanted. Finally she went to the telephone and asked the Geneva exchange to put her through to the Foreign Office in London.

M.I.5 men arrive

The call came through at once and she asked for Mr. Carey-Foster, to find that he was abroad. But she spoke to one of his assistants.

She said she was Mrs. Dunbar, mother-in-law of Donald Maclean and asked if the official to whom she was speaking knew who she was.

He did and she said she had to get into touch with M.I.5 very urgently

Forty minutes later a senior official telephoned to her. She told him that Melinda and the children were missing, that they had gone away for the week-end and had not returned.

He said: "Would you like me to come over to Geneva?" Mrs. Dunbar said she would. He replied that he would be there as soon as possible, that she was not to worry, and that it would be better if she told no one else.

At this point Mrs. Dunbar had not informed the Swiss police, for she felt that it was impera-

WAS SHE THERE?

Territet—the quiet suburb of Montreux where Melinda said she was week-ending

tive that the British authorities who had worked on the earlier Burgess and Maclean disappearance should be told first, and anyhow she was afraid that if she went to police headquarters she would have to explain everything to a junior officer who would possibly never have heard of the Maclean case.

That evening, less than a day after Mrs. Dunbar realised that something had happened to Melinda, two senior M.I.5 officers flew to Geneva, where they arrived early on Tuesday morning.

Waiting for news

They went to the flat in the Rue des Alpes, heard Mrs. Dunbar's story, and, with Swiss police officers, drove off at once to Montreux, where they spent most of the day trying to find either the hotel at which Melinda had said she was to meet her Cairo friend Robin Muir, or the villa where she had expected to spend the week-end.

All Tuesday Mrs. Dunbar waited in agony for news—but there was none. She had with her by now her daughter Harriet

427

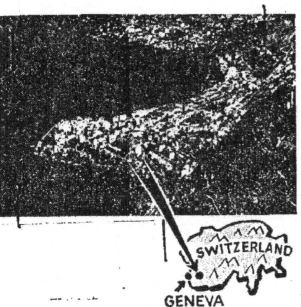

SWITZERLAND

GENEVA

and son-in-law Jay Sheers, who had flown down from Paris.

That night she decided to telephone to her other daughter, Mrs. Catherine Terrell, in New York, to break the sad news to her before she had the shock of reading it in the newspapers—which, however, had not yet got wind of the sensational new development in the Maclean case.

And it was through this perfectly natural telephone message that the news of Melinda's disappearance reached the Press of the world.

For spending the day with Mrs. Terrell when her mother's telephone call came through was a woman friend whose husband was a journalist, working on a small New York newspaper and also as a tipster for one of the big news agencies. That night he telephoned the story to his newspaper and agency. By Wednesday morning the world knew that Melinda Maclean and her three children had vanished.

The immediate result in London was a flood of inquiries at the Foreign Office by journalists seeking confirmation—or denial—of this story from an American

source concerning something that happened in Geneva to an Englishwoman and her three children, particularly as the woman was Mrs. Maclean.

One imagines that the Foreign Office and the security officers pursuing the inquiry would have appreciated a far longer period of secrecy, but as the news had broken this was no longer possible, and a statement giving an accurate and surprisingly full summary of the then known facts was issued from Whitehall.

A Foreign Office spokesman made some extremely interesting comments. He said that it was "entirely a matter for speculation whether Mrs. Maclean had left to join her husband."

He emphasised that she was an "entirely free agent" and was under no obligation to report her movements.

While the disappearance of any British national "was a matter for concern," the British authorities were, in this case, still anxious to acquire "any additional information" about the Burgess-Maclean case, and it was therefore "natural that two security officers"—whose names were not given—should have been sent at once to Switzerland. Finally, there was "no evidence the disappearance was not voluntary."

Word from Melinda?

The first piece of hard information was obtained during that day—Wednesday—when Mrs. Dunbar received a telegram sent to her in Melinda's name. It had been handed in at 11 a.m. in the one-man branch office at Territet, an outlying suburb of Montreux, where Melinda had told her mother she was going to spend the week-end.

Written in a foreign handwriting, it said:

"Terribly sorry delay in contacting you—unforeseen circumstances have arisen am staying here longer please advise schoolboys returning about a week's time—all extremely well—pink rose in marvellous form—love from all—Melinda."

The investigators appear to have missed a most valuable and simple chance of getting some

line on the people behind Melinda's disappearance.

She had told her mother she was going to Territet. Mrs. Dunbar passed on this information at least 24 hours before the telegram was handed in at the very place Melinda had indicated; widespread investigations were being made by the Swiss police and high-ranking British officers; and yet no one seems to have thought of keeping watch in Territet.

There was nothing at all to guarantee that Melinda would in fact go to Territet, and it is unlikely that she did so.

Pattern as before

But already there was a certain similarity in pattern between this and the earlier disappearance of Burgess and Maclean, and it would surely have been well worth while keeping one man in this small suburb where any stranger would be quickly remarked?

The post office clerk—who could not at first be found for he had shut up shop and gone off to work on his farm—at once remembered the dispatch of the telegram, for at that season of the year the traffic at Territet was insignificant.

It had been handed in by a heavily made-up foreign woman who had, presumably unintentionally, drawn attention to herself and the telegram by the fact that it was written in such bad English that even a Swiss clerk had to ask for certain small alterations to be made.

It is unlikely that even if the messenger—and she was certainly nothing more—had been found, she would have led the police to her superiors.

But, with a little foresight, it is possible that valuable information might have been obtained, and it was badly missed.

[World copyright]

| Mr. Tolson |
| Mr. Boardman |
| Mr. Nichols |
| Mr. Belmont |
| Mr. Harbo |
| Mr. Mohr |
| Mr. Parsons |
| Mr. Rosen |
| Mr. Tamm |
| Mr. Sizoo |
| Mr. Winterrowd |
| Telc. Room |
| Mr. Holloman |
| Miss Gandy |

The first
faltering step
to *EXILE*

THE MISSING MACLEANS

ELEVENTH INSTALMENT

By GEOFFREY HOARE

DELETED COPY SENT   C.B. MacDonald
BY LET   JUN 22 1976
PER FOIA REQUEST

RE: DONALD DUART MacLEAN, et al-
    ESPIONAGE - R
    (Bufile 100-374183)

NEWS CHRONICLE
SEPTEMBER 7, 1954
LONDON, ENGLAND

1376

170 SEP   954

429

ONLY three days remained after Melinda returned in that September, 1953, with her mother, Mrs. Dunbar, and the three children, from the holiday in Majorca.

Only three more days in the security and safety of the free world. And on any of them Melinda, by a word, by a gesture, even, could have saved herself and her children.

But she said nothing. She told no one the terrible secret which must have weighed with such crushing torment on her. In fact, the three days passed so busily that even now Mrs. Dunbar is not quite certain exactly what did happen.

One fact has remained firmly fixed in her memory: Melinda tried persistently to persuade her to go away. She had only returned to Geneva from her visit to New York ten weeks before they all went to Majorca. And since Maclean's disappearance she had, except for that absence and another short holiday, been Melinda's inseparable companion and support.

Yet on the Tuesday morning, the day after their return from Majorca, Melinda suggested that it would be a " nice change " if she went over to London. Mrs. Dunbar replied reasonably that she had not the slightest wish to go to London so soon after her return to Geneva.

Then Melinda asked why she did not go to Paris. " Don't you think it would be a good idea if you went to Paris for a little while to buy some new clothes? " she asked.

Mrs. Dunbar pointed out firstly she did not want any clothes and, secondly, Harriet was away from Paris. Melinda nevertheless tried several times to ring up Harriet at her Paris number.

Eventually Mrs. Dunbar said she would be going to Paris " some time after Fergus's birthday " (September 23).

" Oh, that will be too late," replied Melinda.

" Too late for what ? " asked a mystified Mrs. Dunbar.

Melinda did not reply.

Odd ? But not then

Examining this full story of Melinda's last days in Switzerland in the knowledge of what was so soon to happen, one might feel that her behaviour was sufficiently strange to awaken a suspicion that something was wrong, something out of the ordinary was in the air.

Surely her demeanour, her actions, her words were not normal ? The answer is, of course, that for this unhappy, bewildered girl whose life had been so catastrophically overturned and who, for a long period, had been distraught, uncertain, tormented, there was no longer anything deeply unusual in this behaviour.

It must also be remembered that neither Mrs. Dunbar nor anyone else close to Melinda ever had the slightest suspicion that she had been contacted or that she would in any circumstances contemplate going to Donald.

Without any such suspicion all that she did and said had no real significance ; it was merely a symptom of her intense unhappiness and uncertainty.

Nice fresh hair-do

Apart from this and one other strange little conversation, the last three days, Tuesday, Wednesday and Thursday, September 8, 9 and 10, passed rather busily in the normal preoccupations of a family which had just returned from a long summer holiday.

Melinda seemed to be in and out of the flat the whole time, and by the evening was sufficiently tired to go early to bed. Mrs. Dunbar not only did not see very much of her, but, contrary to her usual custom, had little occasion for the long talks they usually had together each night.

One thing that she did struck Mrs. Dunbar as curious and unlike Melinda. On the Thursday she brought back from the dry cleaners three of her summer frocks which she had taken in on the Tuesday.

In the first place, it was unlike Melinda to be so prompt in having her clothes cleaned. Secondly, it was totally unlike her to take her own dresses without asking her mother if she, too, had not something she would like cleaned, especially as they had both come back from their holiday with their dresses crushed.

On the Thursday, too, Melinda spent the afternoon at the beauty parlour having her hair washed, cut and set. There was nothing in this : it was a normal and natural thing for a girl to do, especially on her return from a seaside holiday.

But, again, it was much quicker than one would expect from Melinda who usually took her time about everything, especially about anything connected with her appearance or her clothes.

Added together, in the revealing light of later events, Melinda's actions on her return to Geneva were consistent with those of someone preparing for an important journey. But at the time they appeared entirely ordinary and attracted no attention.

On the Thursday night the last night she spent with her mother, who was also her closest friend in the world, Melinda clearly came very near to breaking down, very near to revealing what was happening.

A cry for advice

Late that night, as they were going to bed, Melinda stood in the doorway between their two rooms " looking ghastly — ill, tired, desperately worried.

Suddenly, and with no connection with what they had been talking about, she said: " Oh, how I wish I had someone to advise me ! "

Mrs. Dunbar had no idea what she meant. The only subject they had discussed that day on which it seemed likely that Melinda could want advice was the disposal of the house at Taitsfield, on which large annual payments had still to be made.

So she replied: " Well, Melinda, I have had certain experience with property in America and although I do not know what happens if England I think I could advise you if you tell me exactly what's worrying you."

Melinda gave her mother one uncomprehending look, shook her head — and went into her bedroom and shut the door.

Was she about to tell her mother of the perilous step she was contemplating ? Had she still not quite decided to obey the summons which had come or which she knew was about to

430

arrive? Was she still in doubt? One just does not know. Her mother had all along been her confidant. She had not wanted to marry Donald before going back to America to tell her mother about him. She insisted on returning to her mother's home in the middle of the war to have her first baby. She called her mother to her when Donald disappeared.

Then came the day

And from that moment Mrs. Dunbar had been at her side constantly and had helped her through all her troubles. The urge to turn to her again must have been almost irresistible, and Melinda must have been desperately torn in heart and mind.

But she held back. Something even stronger than her love for her mother, her love for her own country, her own way of life, was pulling her in another direction, and she dare not speak, for she knew that if she had even hinted that she was about to follow Donald and to take her children with her, Mrs. Dunbar would have immediately mobilised every security force in Europe — and America.

The Friday opened normally, with Melinda appearing no more depressed or preoccupied than usual. After breakfast she went off in her car to the "big" market, which was held twice a week in Geneva. On other mornings she would do the daily shopping at the ordinary "small" market near the flat.

She was gone quite a while and when she returned it was evident that something had happened. She was incandescent with excitement. The die had been cast. Her decision was taken. There were no more doubts.

She hurried into the flat, almost threw down her morning's purchases, and turned excitedly to her mother, to tell her about the "two loveliest things" that had happened to her.

Mrs. Dunbar cannot remember what the second was.

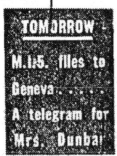

TOMORROW —
M.I.5. flies to
Geneva . . . . .
A telegram for
Mrs. Dunbar

But the first was that a friend of Cairo days called Robin Muir had met her accidentally in the market and invited her and the children to spend a week-end with him and his wife in their villa at Territet.

As she might have difficulty in finding the villa, he had said he would meet her in the lobby of a Montreux hotel—Mrs. Dunbar does not recollect whether Melinda mentioned the hotel by name—at 4.30 that afternoon.

We now know that this "chance meeting with an old friend from Cairo" was probably untrue, anyway to the extent that if indeed it had been someone Melinda had known in her Cairo days who had been selected as the guide to take her to Donald, she knew that there was certainly to be no "week-end with the children at his villa at Territet."

Was she playing a careful and indeed cunning role? It would be so unlike Melinda who, as her mother and close friends have repeatedly stressed to me was not a deceitful person, was on the contrary frank and simple and a poor liar.

Yet, what is one to think? That even at this moment Melinda did not know what she was about to do?

Her immediate actions are capable of two interpretations: Either that she did indeed think she was taking the children to the house of some old friends, or that she was taking them to meet a father they had not seen for months and who had in fact never set eyes on his baby daughter.

For she declared that she must buy "Pinkers" a new coat and some new shoes, and she took the baby and Fergus with her and went off again to the shops.

She returned some time later, showed her mother the things she had bought, put the baby to bed and busied herself about the house—still in a state of some excitement.

She was probably doing her own packing at this time. She had said they must leave at 3 p.m., and then just before luncheon Mrs. Dunbar found that neither she nor Melinda had much money.

She told Melinda to ring up the bank and find out their balance and it was decided that after lunch when the banks reopened Melinda would drive there and cash a cheque.

But after lunch a reaction seemed to set in and long after they had finished Melinda sat at the table, playing restlessly with a half-emptied glass of wine, deep in thoughts which from the look of strain and tension on her face, were far from happy.

Mrs. Dunbar had to remind her that she would be late if she did not hurry, and with a visible effort Melinda shook off her abstraction and drove off to the bank where she cashed a cheque for 700 Swiss francs—at that time roughly £60.

She arrived back just before 3, having paid a garage bill of 50 Swiss francs, and bought some face powder and lipstick, but having forgotten aspirin which Mrs. Dunbar had particularly asked her to buy.

She had also a parcel which she told her mother contained a

431

jersey dress which she had bought, but, most unusually, she did not open this to show it to Mrs. Dunbar.

It is probable from the time she was gone and the things she had to do in it that this dress had been ordered beforehand. Mrs. Dunbar does not think Melinda had had enough time to select and try on a dress of this kind.

An excited flurry

Melinda gave Mrs. Dunbar 200 Swiss francs and probably had around 350 remaining in her purse.

When Melinda returned from her dash to the bank and the shops there was a flurry of excitement. It was already a little after 3—the time they had planned to leave—and they were not nearly ready.

The baby was awakened and dressed in her new little woollen jacket and shoes; the boys put on grey flannel suits; Melinda herself appeared in a black skirt and white blouse over which she wore a three-quarter-length bright blue Schiaparelli coat.

But Mrs. Dunbar was horrified when she saw the skirt. "For Heaven's sake, Melinda," she said, "you can't go away in that dirty skirt."

So Melinda went off to change. Little Donald wanted to take some blue jeans Mrs. Dunbar had brought back from New York for him; and at the last minute she noticed that the baby's favourite doll had been left behind.

At 3.30 they were ready. Mrs.

Dunbar kissed the children goodbye and told Melinda to be careful. Melinda said she would, and repeated that they would be back early on Sunday evening.

There was nothing emotional or agitated in her demeanour. After the flurry and excitement of getting ready, she was calm and almost casual.

In fact, in its ordinariness there was a striking similarity between her departure and that of Donald 27 months earlier; no one could possibly have foretold that, instead of going off to do exactly what she said she was—spend a week-end with friends—she was starting one of the most momentous and dramatic journeys any woman would make: self-chosen exile behind the Iron Curtain.

Her last words to her mother were, in fact, "Would you like me to ring you up when I get there?" Mrs. Dunbar told her not to bother . . .

She took the key

And at 3.30 p.m. on Friday, September 11, Melinda drove off with her three children—taking with her not only the three large keys to the apartment in the Rue des Alpes she was never to see again, but also the only key to the letter box. She was wearing a set of gold clips and pin Mrs. Dunbar bought her in Majorca.

And, hanging over her shoulder, still in the case it had hardly, if ever, left, was the brand new camera Mrs. Dunbar had bought for her.

That was the last glimpse Mrs. Dunbar had of her daughter.

[World copyright]

Mr. Tolson
Mr. Boardman
Mr. Nichols
Mr. Belmont
Mr. Harbo
Mr. Mohr
Mr. Parsons
Mr. Rosen
Mr. Tamm
Mr. Sizo,
Mr. Winterrowd
Tele. Room
Mr. Holloman
Miss Gandy

THE MISSING MACLEANS

TENTH INSTALMENT

Melinda is warned to be ready

by GEOFFREY HOARE

DELETED COPY SENT C.B. MacDonald
BY LETT. JUN 22 1976
PER FOIA REQUL.

RE: DONALD DUART MacLEAN, et al
ESPIONAGE - R
(Bufile 100-374183)

NEWS CHRONICLE
SEPTEMBER 6, 1954
LONDON, ENGLAND

7398

170 SEP 17 1954

OFFICE OF THE LEGAL ATTACHE
AMERICAN EMBASSY
5 5 SEP 20 1954

433

IN some ways the five weeks in Majorca during the summer of 1953, were the happiest Melinda had spent since Maclean left. Cala Ratjada, where she stayed with her mother and children, is a little seaside village some sixty miles from Palma, the capital.

It is on a bay in the lovely rocky eastern coast of the island, and in villas built on the cliff live a small colony of British and American families who have made this charming island their home—anyway, for the summers.

The weather was magnificent and the children had a Heavenly time on the beach and playing in the sea. Melinda appeared to be happy. Although at times nervous and worried she seemed for a time to have shaken off the depression which had obtained so firm a grip on her.

The fair artist

She was a great success and made many friends—as she had also many admirers. Seeing Melinda thaw out in the Majorca sunshine and in the friendliness and admiration which surrounded her, Mrs. Dunbar also began to feel some relief.

At last, she told herself, Melinda was beginning to forget the tragedy which had come into her life, was beginning to forget that she was the wife of the Missing Diplomat, was beginning even, to forget the Diplomat himself.

But events were to prove her wrong. Among the friends they made at Cala Ratjada was an artist, a tall, fair man of about 50. And one day, when they had been at Cala Ratjada a fortnight or so, Melinda said quite suddenly: "How like Donald he is!"

A chance remark

There was indeed a strong resemblance, not only in looks, but also in walk, gesture and voice.

It was one day soon after this that Melinda came back from the beach and, as she stood on the veranda of the house in which they were living, gazing out at the sea, she said, suddenly and with no connection to what she had previously been saying: "He doesn't believe in war either."

At the time Mrs. Dunbar replied, casually, her mind on other things, something like: "Well, lots of people don't believe in war," and gave the matter no further thought.

Later, after Melinda had disappeared, this chance remark assumed great significance.

Melinda was one of the least politically-conscious of women, quite astonishingly so if it is remembered that she had been married for over ten years to a man whose profession was international affairs.

She was rarely, if ever, heard to begin a discussion on any of the great world problems of the day, and if they were brought up in her presence she would reply vaguely and without interest or knowledge.

Innocent words

But if, at the back of her mind, she did store away a few vague unformed views, they were the residue of views she had heard Donald advance—the few phrases or ideas that had stuck, for Donald did the family thinking.

This vital question of "not believing in war," was, however, one of the rare exceptions. She had said it, in quite different circumstances, once before, and little Fergus, watching a school-friend playing rapturously with toy tanks and wooden soldiers, had once said, rather proudly that his daddy was fighting for peace.

It could well be that those few innocent words hide the entire secret of the disappearance of these five human beings, two adults and three children.

But was it by sheer coincidence that Melinda heard some echo of them on the golden sands of Majorca? Or had she already received messages telling her that wherever Donald was and whatever else he might be doing, he was basically still fighting for peace?

There was, however, only one other thing of any significance that happened during the Majorca holiday. One evening, as they were getting ready to go out to dinner, Mrs Dunbar heard Melinda say—again, probably to herself—"Oh, what have I done with Donald's letter?"

It is probable that this was the letter she received in Tatsfield a few weeks after Donald disappeared, and which she always carried with her.

Mother is angry

But there is a vague possibility that Melinda might have received another letter, which she kept secret.

Melinda was obviously contacted several times before the last meeting which resulted in her flight, but it is unlikely that anything was arranged by letter or that anything, at any time, was put in writing.

A few days before they left Majorca Mrs. Dunbar suggested to Melinda that she should write to the garage in Geneva where they had left the car to ask that it be taken to the airport to meet them when they landed. She had also said it would be a help, as they were due to arrive in the late afternoon, if Melinda wrote to the concierge to ask her to buy milk, bread, butter, eggs and the other groceries they would require that evening and the next morning.

The day they were leaving, Mrs. Dunbar found that Melinda had not written, and asked her to send telegrams.

They landed at Cointrin Airport, some 20 minutes from Geneva, around 4.30 p.m. on Monday September 7. There was no car to meet them.

Mrs. Dunbar turned to Melinda. "Did you send the tele—"

Before she could finish her

434

sentence a contrite Melinda broke in. "Oh Mummy! I'm terribly sorry. In the rush to get away I forgot all about it."

For once, the long-suffering Mrs. Dunbar was angry. The children, after their long journey, were tired and a little fretful; they had piles of luggage with them, for in addition to the bags they took, there were the big native-made straw hold-alls they had bought, as well as all kinds of treasures the children had collected.

"Well," she said, "you'd better go and 'phone—quickly."

They sat around in the airport for half an hour before the car arrived, and then when they reached the flat there was, of course, no milk, bread, butter, nothing in fact for the children's supper.

Still contrite, Melinda said she would go and buy them. The children were still unloading the car and leaving bags and suit-cases strewn about the living-room.

Letter in her hand

Melinda went off to the shops. She could have bought everything they needed, not only for that night but for all the next week in about ten minutes, for the shops were just around the corner.

But she was away 50 minutes. When she returned she had not only the packages of groceries, but also a number of letters which she could have collected, either going out or coming back, from the letter box in the hall by the concierge's room.

She dropped the groceries on to the table and all the letters but one on the desk and stood there, with the one remaining letter in her hand, staring at her mother with an extraordinary expression on her face.

Astonishment, apprehension, fear, excitement seemed to follow each other so rapidly that they merged into what was almost a grimace.

'This is it'

"She looked quite awful," said Mrs. Dunbar. But, wise after the event, her mother also now believes that the dominant expression was one of excitement.

"Thinking it over, as I have done hundreds of times, I now feel that Melinda's whole attitude at that moment expressed one thing—'This is it; this is zero hour.'"

At the time all that happened was that Mrs. Dunbar immediately asked what was the matter. Had she received bad news?

"No," said Melinda, pulling herself together. "It's nothing. It's only a letter from the school telling me that opening has been postponed a week and the boys haven't to return until tomorrow week."

This certainly did not seem tragic to Mrs. Dunbar, who in fact remarked that it was rather good news. It would give them time to get the boys ready at leisure and to allow them to settle down a little after the excitements of their holiday.

And, with the litter of un-packed bags all around them, and the need to get the children their evening meal, the episode passed out of her mind, and she did not give it a second thought until several weeks later. But Melinda's behaviour, looked at in retrospect, now became curious. What had happened?

Still no clue

It is possible that Melinda had received some kind of a message either in one of the other letters, or from some contact she had seen while she was out?

Had it been at one of the shops she visited, one of the ordinary shops at which she was accustomed to buy the household goods?

Or had she, during those fifty minutes, called in at some incon-spicuous little place—a tobac-conist's, a stationer's, a bar, a dry cleaner's—which had been opened in Geneva for the express purpose of acting as an accommodation address for a Soviet intelligence organisation and through which Melinda received her instructions?

It could be anything; but we do not know. Melinda's move-ments were, of course, not watched and, despite the exten-sive inquiries made by M.I.5 and the Swiss Police, and other organisations, nothing has been discovered throwing any light on the mystery.

Tortured soul

But one thing is certain: on that evening Melinda had some-how been told that the date of her departure was very near.

It is unlikely that the exact date was given her—any more than Donald and Guy Burgess knew for certain when they drove away from Beaconshaw that evening 27 months earlier that they were leaving never to return.

But she had probably been warned to be ready. And certainly she had been instructed not to say anything to anyone, nothing that could possibly give hint of what she was about to do. From that moment Melinda was a tortured soul.

[World copyright]

THE MISSING MACLEANS

by GEOFFREY HOARE

NINTH INSTALMENT

MRS. DUNBAR returned to Geneva from the United States in May, 1953, and was shocked at the appearance of her daughter Melinda Maclean.

She was whiter than ever, drawn and strained and utterly apathetic. She looked so ill and wretched Mrs. Dunbar asked anxiously if there was anything the matter.

Melinda replied vaguely that there was nothing particularly wrong. She implied that she had been lonely and worried about money—which may have been true but was certainly quite unnecessary—and about the servants.

But Melinda's strange apathy went very deep. Previously full of interest and excitement, even about the plans they were making and particularly about the steps Mrs. Dunbar was to take about getting back her American passport and obtaining American nationality for the children. Melinda now showed no interest in all that Mrs. Dunbar had done.

Untouched presents

She did not even trouble to read any of the voluminous correspondence Mrs. Dunbar had with solicitors and the State Department.

Similarly, although expressing great gratitude, she made only a perfunctory inspection of the delightful clothes, dresses, underclothes and nightdresses Mrs. Dunbar had brought back

for her, and most of them remained in their original packages — in which, it is presumed, Melinda took them away with her.

And she had particularly asked that her mother should buy her these things, which were, she said, much better and cheaper in New York than in Geneva.

During the previous months much discussion had taken place on the question of a job for Melinda. She had no idea what she wanted to or could do, but she was insistent that she should do something. At one time she had been interested in photography and Mrs. Dunbar thought she might try to become a specialist in photography of children.

The new dress

So Mrs. Dunbar bought Melinda a Rollieflex camera. This, too, remained untouched in its case.

But life went on. Melinda had made new friends during Mrs. Dunbar's absence and went out to cocktail parties and dinners more frequently than she had since her Cairo days. But she in no way regained her spirits.

Another little incident, strangely reminiscent of a similar happening in Washington, occurred soon after Mr. Dunbar's return.

Geneva is by no means a "dressy" place, and at most of the dinner parties Melinda attended the men wore day suits or at the most dinner jackets and black ties, and the women simple evening frocks.

But for one party to which she was invited Melinda was asked to wear full evening dress, as some of the other women had new ball dresses which they wished to show off.

Melinda mentioned this to Mrs. Dunbar, who, with her usual generosity, insisted that Melinda should immediately have a suitable dress sent from

Paris. Together they tel to their Paris dressmar in a few days the dress

Melinda tried it on; lovely; she "adored it, hung in a wardrobe. went to the party in a black frock. And the ne still unworn, was the o Dunbar found when s back, a month after had disappeared, to clos apartment.

All this time nothing which, even in the lig that she then knew, Mr could afterwards rem having any significance

The hot weather can June 10 Melinda bo tickets for Majorca. T term ended on June 30 were all due to leave t ing day. A letter was MacKillop (the Americ who had invited them t telling him they would ing at Cala Ratjada o

As the time drew boys' excitement rose loved the seaside and talked of little else.

Melinda appeared p and quiet, but also be looking forward change.

Then, two or three o the end of the month, happened. What it w not know. But one Dunbar, who was an bad sleeper, was rea bed long after midn she heard Melinda w lessly about in the n

Sleeple night

So she got up and see her. "What's Melinda?" she ask you sleep? Have yo on your mind?"

Melinda looked at in silence for a fe Then she said: "Oi don't know quite ho but I've changed r feel I need some r and I want to take up to Saanenmös weeks before we go

Mrs. Dunbar wa She and Melinda k well how excitedly been looking forwar and although they skiing, this was l there was no sno

436

Mr. Boardman
Mr. Nichols
Mr. Belmont
Mr. Harbo
Mr. Mohr
Mr. Parsons
Mr. Rowen
Mr. Tamm
Mr. Sizoo
Mr. Winterrowd
Tele. Room
Mr. Holloman
Miss Gandy

A suddenly changes
oliday plans

THE SKI-ING VILLAGE OF SAANENMOSER
Why did Melinda go back in high summer?

telephoned
aker and
s arrived.

, it was
. It was
Melinda
a simple
new dress,
one Mrs.
the went
Melinda
se up the

happened
at of all
s. Dunbar
ember as

e and on
ught the
The school
and they
the follow-
written to
n friend
Majorca)
be arriv-
July 2

near, the
gh they
for weeks

reoccupied
seemed to
to the

ays before
something
us, we do
ight Mrs.
extremely
ing in her
ht when
king rest-
t room.

ss

went in to
the matter,
. "Can't
something

her mother
moments.
Mummy, I
to tell you,
mind. I
untain sir
he children
for two
Majorca."

astounded
only too
e boys had
to Majorca,
d enjoyed
b summer.
and there

would be practically nothing for
them to do at Saanenmöser.

Further, Melinda knew only too
well that Mrs. Dunbar herself
loathed the mountains.

So Mrs. Dunbar said:
"There's no need for you to go
to Majorca if you don't want to.
But Fergus and Donald will be
broken-hearted if they don't go.
You go on up to the mountains
and I'll take the children to
Majorca."

But Melinda refused this com-
promise: she wanted the children with her, she said.

Mother and daughter talked
until the early morning, but
Melinda, although apologetic and
distressed, was determined and,
as happened so often, she got
her own way.

The children's disappointment
when they were told of the
change of plans was pathetic—
but even this did not influence
Melinda. That morning she went
to the travel agency and can-
celled their bookings and wired
to MacKillop in Majorca to tell
him they would not be coming
until much later.

And then, on the morning of
July 3 Melinda bundled the
children into her car and drove
off for the hills: she intended to
stay at Saanenmöser for at least
a fortnight, she said as they left.

The change in Melinda's plans

had been very sudden. She had
written to Harriet only on June
24—the last letter Harriet
received from her—and had not
mentioned the holidays, neither
to speak of preparations for going
to Majorca nor of any intention
she had of not going.

It was a hurried gossipy letter
concerned mainly with Harriet
and her second child which had
been born a few weeks earlier.

Sister is alarmed

There was only one thing of
significance in the letter. Melinda
wrote: "Be prepared for a long
visit from me next fall," which
would seem at least an indication
that she had at that moment no
thought that by "next fall" she
would be in a place from which
visits to Paris were impossible.

On July 3, soon after Melinda
had left with the children for
Saanenmöser, Harriet telephoned
from Paris to know what had
happened; she had expected to
see them in Paris on their way
through to Spain.

When she heard that Melinda
had changed her mind and gone
to the mountains, she was

definitely alarmed. She had a
premonition that something was
wrong and contemplated flying
to Switzerland to talk to Melinda.
She did in fact telephone her at
Saanenmöser, but it was an un-
satisfactory and inconclusive conversation which served only to
heighten Harriet's uneasiness.

But her baby was only a few
weeks old and the nurse had just
left and it was impossible for her
to leave Paris.

But on July 8, five days after
she drove off saying she would be
away a fortnight, Melinda returned to Geneva. She told her
mother the weather in the mountains had been bad: there had
been no sun and the atmosphere
was heavy, and altogether
Saanenmöser had been "dull and
boring."

Boat at last

So she had brought the children back and suggested that they
should all go off to Majorca. But
Swiss ski-ing resorts are essen-
tially for the winter and all these
things Melinda could well have
guessed beforehand.

Mrs. Dunbar, delighted to have
her family back and pleased at
the prospect of finally starting
the seaside holiday, did not question her.

She was by now accustomed to
the changing moods of her unhappy daughter and was concerned only in seeing that
everything possible was done to
make her happy, to help her to
forget the terrible tragedy which
had shattered her life.

The next day Melinda went to
rebook the tickets for Majorca.
This, unfortunately, was not
easy; it was by now the height
of the holiday season and boats
were already full. It was not
possible to obtain passages for
the next fortnight, and it was not
until July 23, three weeks after
they had originally intended to
begin their holiday, that Melinda,
her three children and her
mother left Geneva.

[World copyright]

ON MONDAY
Did Melinda
receive a "come
now" letter?

437

THE MISSING MACLEANS
by GEOFFREY HOARE

EIGHTH INSTALMENT

IN the summer of 1952 Melinda Maclean and her family spent a few days in Paris. Then, in the new car Mrs. Dunbar had bought her, she drove to Normandy for a holiday.

The house they had rented at Glanville bore the grand name of Le Manoir de Madame des Vaux and was in delightful countryside a few miles inland from Deauville.

But it rained nearly every day and Melinda had neither the sunshine nor the rest her doctor had prescribed.

My wife and I drove down to spend the week-end and found it difficult to revive any of her real gaiety.

Soon after that, with the weather growing steadily worse, she and her mother decided to cut short the holiday and they returned to Paris.

There again we saw a good deal of Melinda, and there it was for the first time that she said she was sure Donald was behind the Iron Curtain.

She had nothing to go on, but somehow, she said, she just knew.

Now for a new life

So she had really decided to remake her life. She was going to take her mother and the children to Geneva, put the children into school, find a flat, and then go over to England to try to get rid of Beaconshaw, sell Donald's car, talk to solicitors seriously about a divorce, and take steps to get back her American passport.

And she must find a job. Romanticising herself somewhat, as I later discovered, she drew a graphic picture of the terrible plight she would be in should her mother die. She and the children, she told me, were entirely dependent upon Mrs. Dunbar and would very likely starve because her mother's money died with her, as it were.

This was nonsense. It was true that she and the children were living on Mrs. Dunbar, for Maclean had left her nothing but debts—the £2,000 repaid the advance on Beaconshaw—and she had received not a penny from the Foreign Office since he was "suspended" on June 1, 1951.

But she had a small scheme of her own, she would at some time or other come into more money from a trust fund established by her grandfather, and when her mother died she would be reasonably comfortably off.

That was clearly looking into the future. The fact remains that, most fortunately for her and her children, financial worries at least were spared her.

Other worries persisted and were indeed more real to her. She felt the children needed a "father." It would be bad for them continually to be brought up in a "man-less" home.

Would she remarry?

I suggested that when she had divorced Donald she could easily remarry.

"Who would marry a notorious woman like me with three small children?" she asked.

The answer was obvious: lots of men would be only too delighted to marry her. For Melinda, although she had aged some ten years in the months since Maclean went off into the unknown, was still an exceedingly attractive girl who, if she could only emerge from the black depression which gripped her so relentlessly, would look far younger than her 36 years.

She had many most admirable qualities—and her natural gaiety and spontaneity would soon return.

But, no. She was convinced that her marital life was definitely over never to begin again. The only future for her lay in finding a job; but what could she do? This was a problem, for she had never done any real work.

The next day, September 3, 1952, she left for Geneva, driving her mother, the three children and their devoted English nurse in her new American car.

It is another example of the contradictions in Melinda that this apparently frail, sick girl could quite easily drive the long and sometimes arduous 12-hour journey from Paris to Geneva, mainly in pouring rain, in one lap.

Then, after a few days, she went with considerable trepidation to see the headmaster of the international school to arrange about sending the boys there—and to tell him who they were. Afterwards, she wrote to her sister:

"It was absolute agony telling him about Donald, but I felt of course I had to do it."

And at the same time she had the difficult, delicate task of explaining to Fergus and Donald Jnr. what had happened to their father.

The boys started school, which they liked very m[uch] Melinda looked round [...] She was also looking [...] and without much sensa[...] tion for the job whic[...] enable her to start a [...] But although physic[...] picked up a little, spiri[...] was still very low and [...] me in the middle of S[...]

"I feel so completely [...] since arriving here and [...] how I can summon up [...] it takes to start a new [...]

She look[ed] better

At the beginning of [...] Melinda and her fami[...] into a little apartment [...] found in the Rue des A[...] most pleasant part of [...] within sight of the la[...] and with a little park [...] which the children co[...]

I was in Geneva at [...] and went to see her in [...] setting.

Melinda was a little [...] little elated about the [...] felt it would make a [...] ference to their life and [...] the move as a sort of [...] "settling down" in Ge[...]

I thought she look[ed] better than she had [...]

438

village that held

...ret

...ny months when she came in, ...le cheeks a little flushed, arms ...ll of flowers, vegetables and ...uit from the market—the first ...rchases for the new flat.

One of her most endearing ...alities was an enthusiasm for ...le which fate's savage blows ...ver entirely diminished. She ...as always prepared to make the ...est of circumstances and to re-...rd each new page as the open-...ng of a better and brighter ...hapter.

The new flat, which was some-...hat small, a little dark, and ...lled with typical "furnished ...partment" furniture and fit-...ngs, could have been intensely ...epressing. Melinda refused to ...et it add to her depression and ...ndeed seemed to regard it as a ...ort of challenge.

She would find something good ...bout it, and wrote to her sister, who had a most delightful flat ...n Paris: "We simply adore our ...partment. This is the first time ...have lived in the middle of a city for years and I simply love ...t. Never mention the country ...o me again except for week-ends and holidays."

Poor Melinda! With that spirit ...he really did deserve something ...etter of life.

Last time I saw her

We said good-bye to her in Geneva and arranged that she should come to stay with us in Paris. But although we wrote to each other a few times she did not come, and that was, in fact, the last time I saw her. The next time I went to Geneva it was to report her disappearance.

After she had fully settled down in Geneva, her mother per-suaded her to take a long rest, and except for a few days in Paris with her sister, Harriet, who had "never seen Melinda so low in spirits," she spent most of November and December in England, having left the children with her mother in Geneva.

In England, she stayed with friends, went to London to see

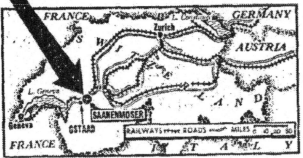

HERE THEY WENT TO SKI

A good spot for contacting someone farther east?

her doctor, her solicitors and her bankers.

She made a beginning with all the things she had intended to do, but made no great progress with any of them. But she en-joyed herself and, as she wrote, "saw almost everybody I ever knew and had quite a whirl."

A happier year?

She returned to Geneva two days before Christmas, and then, on January 1 wrote to Harriet:

"Thank God for a new year. I couldn't have been happier to see 1932 go. Mother and I cele-brated quietly with a bottle of champagne and a miniature log fire, and in our strange optimistic way felt that perhaps 1953 might be better for us all.

"We survived Christmas once more. I am really getting to dread it, and Mother and I could hardly wait to throw away all Christmas decorations; only the Christmas tree remains. Next year I am going to send the boys away with their school friends on a ski-ing trip."

The next few months passed quietly, and, so far as one knew at the time, uneventfully. Mrs. Dunbar left Geneva on January

20 for the United States and did not return to Switzerland until three and a half months later.

In the fuller knowledge which we now have of Melinda's dis-appearance, this period assumes an importance which it did not appear to hold at the time.

In late February or early March Melinda took the children to Saanenmöser, a mountain resort close to Gstaad, where she joined an English friend and her two little girls for a fortnight's ski-ing. Soon after she got back to Geneva she wrote to Harriet:

"I am in a dismally unstable state and have the horrid feel-ing almost anything might push me over the precipice. If I can only hang on for another year."

There was no explanation of this cryptic and, one now feels, significant little passage, sand-wiched, with no further com-ment, between inquiries after Harriet's new baby and informa-tion about Melinda's youngest child.

The visit to Saanenmöser, to which she was to return so mysteriously four months later, may have been extremely im-portant.

"It is a tiny village with three or four hotels and half a dozen villas in a long smooth valley where there is excellent ski-ing. It is not widely known; it is quiet, discreet and within easy reach of Geneva, Montreux and other cities. It is possible that it was there that the first tenta-tive approach to Melinda may have been made.

Soon after Mrs. Dunbar and Melinda had moved to Geneva, they received a letter from an American friend named Douglas MacKillop, who had settled in Majorca.

Surprised mother

If they would like an excellent seaside holiday, he wrote, he would be delighted to take them all as paying guests during the summer.

Before Mrs. Dunbar left for America she and Melinda had not reached a decision. Early in May Mrs. Dunbar reached Paris on her way back from the United States. She telephoned to Melinda in Geneva and dur-ing their conversation Melinda told her mother that she thought it would be an excellent idea if they accepted MacKillop's invitation. This, coming out of the blue, somewhat surprised Mrs. Dunbar.

[World copyright]

TOMORROW
Melinda suddenly changes her holiday plans

439

When DONALD first spoke of COMMUNISM

MCLEAN'S behaviour in Cairo became so outrageous that Melinda besought the Ambassador to let her husband return to London for psychiatric treatment.

In May, 1950, he flew home and shortly afterwards Melinda and her mother took the children for a holiday in Spain.

Early in September, when they had been apart for nearly four months, Melinda received a most curious letter from her husband. It was in some way a letter of renunciation, suggesting that he was not the man for her, and that they would be well advised to part.

On receiving this letter Melinda decided to end her Spanish holiday. She took her mother and her children to Paris and flew over to London to see him.

The talks she had in England with him, with some of his relatives, and with the psychiatrist were probably the most momentous Melinda had ever had, for they again changed the course of her life.

TOGETHER AGAIN

She was asked and advised to resume ordinary married life with him. After acute heart-searchings, Melinda agreed.

They spent a fortnight together in London before Donald decided that they would live together again. Melinda returned to Paris to fetch the children.

They decided they would live

Mocked at himself

in the country near enough to London for Donald to go up and down to the Foreign Office each day, but far enough away so that if he were to reach home in reasonable time for dinner there could be no loitering in bars.

Five days before Christmas, 1950, they moved into Beaconshaw, in the little village of Tatsfield, not far from Westerham, in Kent.

OUTBURST

The first two or three months at Beaconshaw were among the happiest in Melinda's married life. But by the spring Maclean began first to miss the early train, and then to miss the train altogether and spend the night in town.

Early in May, Melinda's sister Harriet and her husband Jay Sheers came over from Paris to spend a few days at Beaconshaw, and it was during this week-end that Maclean revealed to some extent what he was thinking and feeling in an extraordinary conversation with her and her husband.

First, he openly supported Communism, and although he did

not actually say so in as many words, suggested that he was a Communist.

Harriet did not at the time take this outburst seriously: in the past he had frequently teased her and she felt he might be doing so again. But later on this conversation took on a new and extremely important light.

Then Maclean took Jay Sheers to have a drink in the local pub, and there he railed bitterly at his life and his job; he mocked at himself as a sheep amongst hordes of other sheep, going off to London every day with his black hat and neat black suit and little black brief case. He said that he was sick of it all and longed to "cut adrift."

The next day, however, Maclean seemed his normal self.

And in London Maclean was impressing his friends with an unaccustomed serenity as he went through the daily routine of work at his Foreign Office desk, luncheon parties and even occasional drunken evenings. But the end was now very near.

> On May 25, 1951, Maclean and Burgess disappeared. The story of that extraordinary night was recounted in an earlier instalment. TODAY is told how Melinda gradually realised the truth

DONALD had be when Christ Christmas witho New Year.

It was about this time to accept the fact that he

The months of suspense were changing into no less unhappy months of uncertainty: what should she do for the best?

She could not make up her mind. She remained constantly loyal to him, so far a the outside world was concerned, but did she still lov him?

Later events seem to me t prove that Melinda never reall stopped loving him entirel but there is no doubt that fro early 1952 onwards she oft said she no longer loved hi and undoubtedly at the tin she thought this was the ca

In the spring she spent th weeks in a London hospit where she underwent a min operation. During these ratl tedious weeks she talk freely to a friend.

Melinda admitted ope: that she was no longer in l with Maclean and intended

440

INDA accepts it— will not return

gone seven months
came, the first
him, and then the

Melinda began definitely
ld not return.

rce him and try to remake
life. Around this time
my wife and I saw
inda several times, to-
er and separately, and we
e left in no doubt at all
she had decided to end
chapter of her life.
I can't tell you how glad I
this façade of a marriage.
ver," she said. . .
ut what was she to do?
ther she nor anyone else
w what had happened to
clean or where he was.

Life was grim

As a start, Melinda decided
would take steps to regain
American nationality. Then
e would return to New York,
least for a time, where she
t it would be easier to ob-
a divorce.
But for the moment all this
merely theoretical.

PART OF A LETTER WHICH MACLEAN WROTE TO MELINDA WHILE UNDERGOING PSYCHIATRIC TREATMENT IN LONDON

THE WHOLE PASSAGE READS: I am so grateful to you my sweet for taking all you have had to put up with without hating me. I am still rather lost, but cling to the idea that you do want me to be cured and come back.

Melinda was in no shape,
physical or mental, to make
any decisive move in any
direction.
Life at Beaconshaw was
grim and difficult, for it was
definitely a house that needed
a man, and she became more
depressed, more unhappy,
more worried as the days
passed.
She was like a patient after
a long and wasting illness
who simply could not gather
strength again. Her mother
tried to persuade her to go to
Paris for a holiday, leaving the
children with her at Beaconshaw, but Melinda would not
go.
Her baby daughter Melinda,
likened by little Fergus to a
pink rose and henceforth called
"Pinkers," was growing into
a beautiful child and, with
Fergus and Donald, was her
joy and helped her to retain
her sanity and a precarious
grip on life.

441

Still no news

But the weeks passed and still she was unable to emerge from the bottomless pit of depression into which she had sunk. She went back to her doctor, and this time he told her frankly that she had to go away.

"You are living in the past," he said, "and it's terribly bad for you. You are wearing yourself out with anxiety and worry. What you need more than anything is a rest, a change and some sunshine. Go abroad."

Melinda agreed. She knew that was what she longed for. But she still could not make up her mind to do anything about it.

And in a way, I suppose, she felt that she should remain in England so that she could be at hand if there were any developments if M.I.5 obtained any news of Maclean. May came round again with the first anniversary of his disappearance.

A move at last

And then Mrs. Dunbar took charge. She reminded Melinda that something would soon have to be done about the children. Fergus would be eight years old in September and after that could no longer go to the kindergarten school in Sevenoaks he and five-year-old Donald were attending.

Impressed by her mother's arguments, Melinda agreed to go abroad—but at first only for a holiday: she wanted to return to Beaconshaw.

But her mother urged her to take a broader view of their situation. Life for all of them would be far easier abroad, and, whatever Melinda herself might have desired, it would obviously be better for the children.

Mrs. Dunbar herself would really have preferred to return to her own country, but Melinda would not hear of that: the United States was far too far away.

Talk with M.I.5

Paris was the next suggestion. Both Melinda and her mother would have liked to live in Paris but it was expensive and neither of them quite liked the idea of a French school for the boys. Finally, on Mrs. Dunbar's proposal, it was decided that after a holiday in France they would go to Geneva to live and the boys would attend the excellent international school there.

Melinda's brother-in-law Jay Sheers, found them a farmhouse in Normandy where they could be reunited for the summer.

A few days before Melinda and her family were due to leave, the senior M.I.5 investigator telephoned to Mrs. Dunbar at Beaconshaw and said he would like to talk to her. They met in London, and he took her to a café. She had imagined he would have something to tell her, but his information was all negative.

Mrs. Dunbar asked for assurances that if anything was learned, any discovery made, she and Melinda would be immediately informed, wherever they were. He said: "I will get in touch with the Maclean family."

This by no means satisfied Mrs. Dunbar. She pointed out that, as Donald's wife, Melinda had the right to be informed immediately there were any developments.

"You must certainly communicate with her first," she insisted. And although she received no definite undertaking on this point Mrs. Dunbar went off to join Melinda and the children with a slight feeling of reassurance.

Mother was hopeful

Neither Melinda nor, she had now learned, M.I.5 had heard anything more from or about Maclean, and although she presumed a search of some kind was still continuing, the authorities no longer seemed to be particularly interested.

It should now be possible to induce Melinda herself to forget all about it and try seriously to remake her life. But later, after Melinda had disappeared, she reproached herself and the security authorities for this lack of foresight.

"I was Melinda's best protection," she said to me. "I was usually with her and would never have left her at all had I thought there was any danger that Donald would try to contact her. But why didn't M.I.5 tell me there was even an outside chance of her being contacted?

"If they had warned me, I would have done anything to stop her going, from taking a step which can only mean unhappiness for her and for my grandchildren."

[World copyright]

TOMORROW

The fateful journey to Geneva

442

Mr. Tolson	
Mr. Boardman	
Mr. Nichols	
Mr. Belmont	
Mr. Harbo	
Mr. Mohr	
Mr. Parsons	
Mr. Rosen	
Mr. Tamm	
Mr. Sizo	
Mr. Wintercrowd	
Tele. Room	
Mr. Hollman	
Miss Gandy	

The MISSING MACLEANS by Geoffrey HOARE

SIXTH INSTALMENT

THE early years of Melinda's married life were spent peacefully enough, if that adjective is applicable to war-time London.

Melinda and Maclean were bombed out of two flats, but although they very nearly lost their lives in the first incident, after one night in an air-raid shelter, Melinda refused to "take cover" again.

In 1944, however, a new stage of Melinda's life opened, for in April Maclean was appointed acting First Secretary to the British Embassy in Washington.

Melinda was overjoyed at the appointment, both for the promotion it meant for him, and the opportunity it gave her of returning to her own country.

Apart

After a few days in New York, where Maclean met Mrs. Dunbar and Melinda's sisters for the first time and created a highly favourable impression, he left Melinda at her mother's house—where she remained except for one week until her first baby was born—and went on to Washington.

Melinda did not go to live with him there because of the difficulty in finding a suitable house or apartment.

War-time Washington was impossibly overcrowded and his excuse that he could not find anywhere for them to live was, on the surface, plausible—but only just. He himself managed quite happily to live in the apartment of a colleague, leaving Melinda to her own devices in New York.

As all she had to do, as the weeks went by, was to await the birth of her child, it was not a particularly gay time for her.

No money

Maclean always extraordinarily casual about money, rarely sent any to Melinda the whole time she was in New York although he knew he was placing her in the position she detested of having to live off her mother.

The history of their married life is full of occasions on which he left Melinda virtually stranded without money. It was not really that he was mean. Nor does there seem to be any definite connection with the fact that he was always hard-up.

His curious attitude towards the financial side of his married life sprang from a deeper "the world owes me something" outlook towards life at large, and which made many people think that he was spoiled—as in fact he was.

On September 22, 1944, Melinda went into hospital where by a Cæsarean operation her child, Fergus, was born the following day. She and Maclean were delighted and he went back to Washington, where he eventually found an apartment.

New job

He returned to New York in the middle of December and took Melinda and the baby back to Washington two days before Christmas. They lived there for three and a half years, with visits to New York and the east coast for holidays.

The British Embassy in 1945 was still understaffed and overworked, and Donald Maclean was rapidly making a name for himself: from acting First Secretary he became acting Counsellor and head of Chancery.

But in their own intimate life they were far from happy. In June, 1946, Melinda went again to New York and there, on July 27, her second child, Donald Marling, was born. And then after another two years in Washington, Maclean was appointed to Cairo. They sailed for England at the beginning of September, 1948, for home leave before going on to their new post—and the next and supremely important stage in their life together.

At dinner

It was in London that I met them first. I was on leave from the Middle East and one night Clare, my wife, and I were invited to dine at the house of the then head of the Foreign Office department which deals with the Middle East.

It was a party of 12 people and we all knew each other, except Melinda. At dinner I sat next to this delicate-complexioned, soft-voiced little American girl and sensed that in this gathering of people who had been in or had some connection with the Middle East Melinda felt herself rather out of her depth.

I found her utterly charming and with that kind of fragility and defencelessness which made nearly all men feel they wanted to protect her.

After dinner Melinda, Maclean and I sat together and continued to talk about Egypt, and although Maclean—a tall, rather remote but by no means unfriendly figure — showed no marked enthusiasm, I felt that he too was pleased with his new appointment. They seemed a

"NEWS CHRONICLE" London 8-31-54

RE: DONALD D. MacLEAN, ET AL, ESPIONAGE-R.

1398
5 5 SEP 20 1954

DELETED COPY SENT C. B. MacDonald
BY LETTER JUN 22 1976
PER FOIA REQUEST

1 100-397
NOT RECORDED
170 SEP 17 1954

443

Those Cairo parties: Maclean begins to crack up

THE MACLEANS' HOUSE IN CAIRO
A shadow over the gay life

harmonious couple, and my wife and I were happy at the thought that we had made two extremely pleasant new friends. Our farewell to them had been "See you soon in Cairo."

Soon after this Maclean and Melinda went off to Cairo and I returned to Beirut, and it was not until the following March that I arrived in Cairo.

Neighbours

The next day I received a message from Melinda, welcoming me to Cairo and inviting me to cocktails that evening. The Macleans were living in a large, delightful house in Gezireh, furnished and kept up by the Office of Works. A staff of four excellent Berberine servants and an English governess for the children helped to make life smooth-running and pleasant.

I found Melinda on top of the world. She still adored Cairo, and had, probably for the first time in her married life, emerged from her protective shell.

Maclean, after about six months in Egypt, was doing exceptionally well at the Embassy, and he too appeared at this time to be enjoying his new post.

Soon after this meeting my wife joined me in Cairo and some friends of ours at the Embassy lent us their house, which was a few doors away from that occupied by the Macleans.

Dislike

We met the Macleans frequently at the endless round of Cairo parties, and on the rare evenings when neither of us had an engagement we would dine together and play family bridge. It was at this stage of their life that we got to know them well and our liking for them increased.

It soon emerged that Maclean was developing a deep dislike for Egypt.

He disliked the intense social life and the feeling of imprisonment given by a city from which there seemed little escape, and the contrast between the shocking poverty of 95 per cent. of the population and the arrogant, ostentatious wealth of the small ruling class minority outraged his liberal principles.

The work of a British diplomat was complicated by the difficulties raised daily by an inefficient Egyptian Government seeking in the still unresolved "Palestine war" a means of distracting attention from its own extraordinary shortcomings and deflecting to the British a public unpopularity which should have been its own.

British policy at that period was the traditional one of—doing nothing, of sitting back and seeing what would happen, of "non-interference" tainted by the fact that our diplomatic influence and the presence of our troops in the Canal Zone constituted at least a passive interference.

Remote

Maclean objected strongly to this policy. He felt that as we could not escape from the predominant position in Egypt, which our previous status there had given us, we should accept our responsibilities and try to persuade the rulers of Egypt to institute the reforms which alone, in his opinion, could save the country from Communism.

And, except to stress its dangers, that was all I ever heard him say about Communism. Nor, in the course of those frequent evenings together, did I ever know him to drink too much.

A picture of him at that time would show a tall, fair, rather carelessly-dressed man of thirty-six, slightly remote, a little too restrained, sitting low in an armchair with one lanky leg crossed over the other and the free foot constantly jerking up and down, commenting with cynical humour on the stupidity and obtuseness of most of his fellows.

Mocking

His relations with Melinda appeared entirely amicable, if slightly condescending, slightly mocking, for she clearly took no interest in and had no knowledge of the political and social problems which we discussed in the intervals between hands of bridge.

Melinda was on the whole gay and unconcerned by his mockery. How far she had come, this little American girl who only two or three years before in her native Washington had to be cajoled into receiving two or three guests, was shown about this time when she entertained the Duke of Edinburgh. He was on a visit to Cairo and was staying for some days at the British Embassy.

Melinda was asked at short notice to organise a "young people's party" for him. It took place at the Macleans' house in Gezireh, with Melinda as hostess. Twelve members of Cairo's "younger set" were invited to dine with the Duke and other guests came in afterwards. They played slightly juvenile games—such as "murder"—and the party was a great success.

At the end of the summer I left Cairo again. When I got back the following February I heard rather odd stories about Maclean. His antipathy to his life in Egypt was increasing to such an extent, it was said, that he had begun to drink too much.

There had so far been no scandal and, at any rate officially, the Embassy knew nothing about it, but his friends were alarmed.

Scenes

It would be ridiculous to call him an habitual drunkard. I never saw him anything but sober. But from time to time during his life he had been known to seek refuge from problems that were too much for him in a spell of reckless drinking.

His drinking had begun early. There is a letter to him in Paris

477

from Melinda before they were married, in which she writes:

"If you do feel an urge to have a drinking orgy why don't you have it at home—so at least you will be able to get safely to bed?"

I left Cairo again at the beginning of March and by the time I returned at the beginning of May the end of his career in Egypt was within sight.

There had already been two incidents of which a certain number of people knew, and several very unpleasant domestic and more private scenes.

The first incident was relatively unimportant. After two cocktail parties Maclean, instead of going home, had wandered off and had been found shoeless on a bench in the Esbekieh Gardens.

The second was far more serious.

Dangerous

Melinda had hired a picturesque wide-sailed felucca to take some friends up the Nile to Helouan. The wind dropped and the trip, instead of taking two hours, took eight. And Maclean became dangerously drunk.

At one point, in a fit of mad rage, he seized Melinda round the neck and might have strangled her had the others not intervened.

When they reached Helouan at 2 a.m. a ghaffir, or watchman, challenged them with an antiquated rifle. Maclean wrested

the rifle from the ghaffir and began to swing it wildly round his head.

One of the guests, also a Secretary at the Embassy, tried to restrain Maclean, but in their struggle they both fell down the bank—and the other man broke his leg.

What story was told at the Embassy is not known. But the extraordinary feature of this escapade is that it seemed to do no harm to Maclean's career.

And this is true, also, of the final episode, the culminating incident in his 18 months' tour of office as Counsellor and head of Chancery.

Sick leave

It occurred nearly two months later, when Melinda was again pregnant.

On a two-day "binge" he and a friend entered a flat belonging to a girl who worked at the U.S. Embassy, drank what they could find and then proceeded to break up the furniture.

The next morning Melinda and Maclean had a heart-to-heart talk, after which, with a loyalty which even his outrageous behaviour had not shaken, she went to see his Ambassador.

She told him that Donald was ill, was suffering from a nervous breakdown and must be given sick leave to return to London to see his own doctor at once.

And it is, one can only presume, on the strength of Maclean's exceptional qualities and the excellent work he had done—continued to do, it appears from official statements, even at a time when he was drinking so heavily that he was becoming notorious—that this permission was immediately given.

[World copyright]

TOMORROW
THE MARRIAGE HEADS FOR THE ROCKS

The honeymoo
escape from Fi

FIFTH INSTALMENT

SNOW lay thick in Paris that evening in December, 1939, when Melinda first met, at the Café Flore, the man she was to marry.

She had been in Paris more than a year desultorily studying at the Sorbonne but mostly savouring the Left Bank life that still went on although war had come.

The tall, fair young Englishman was introduced to her by an American friend, a writer named Bob McAlmon.

In comes Donald

Just over a year after Melinda had arrived in Paris, war had come again to Europe. The first wild excitement had passed by December, the flurry of mobilisation and the chaos of hastily organised civil defence had died away, and France settled down to cynical comments on the phoney war. By this time the Latin Quarter, curiously unchanged by events which only very far-sighted

people then realised heralded the end of an epoch, had reverted to its normal state of multilingual ebullience

The cafés were as crowded as ever; the streets just as full. To Melinda's regret her 19-year-old sister Harriet had been called home by anxious parents, but at the age of 23 she was mistress of her own destinies and was determined to stay on as long as she could

As Maclean stood inside the dark-curtained glass door, wiping snow from his face and hair, looking round the packed, smoky room in search of familiar faces, he noticed Melinda sitting with a group of friends

He knew her well by sight, for the Latin Quarter is a curiously small world, but he had somehow never met her. He spoke to the man who was with him and they began to push their way through the crush, bandying greetings with nearly everyone there, for Maclean, too, was a popular figure in the heterogeneous society of St. Germain des Prés.

They stood by the table occupied by Melinda and her entourage and vaguely through the babble of talk going on at top speed all around her, Melinda heard McAlmon introducing "my friend, Donald Maclean."

Within a matter of days they became inseparable — but the initiative came from Donald. He "saw her first" as it were; he sought the introduction; he made the running.

That she liked him, enjoyed his company, admired his intelli-

gence, his knowledge, his savoir-faire, is undeniable. For Maclean, although he spent his nights in the cafés and boîtes of the Latin Quarter, where art in any form took precedence over world affairs, where promise was as important as accomplishment, where talk was all, was in many respects a visitor from another world.

Already he was a hard-working and extremely competent diplomat — using that rather loose description to indicate a member of the British Foreign Service — and, at 26, already climbing the ladder of which the topmost rungs were labelled "His Britannic Majesty's Minister Plenipotentiary and Ambassador Extraordinary to Paris . . . to Moscow . . . to Washington."

And so he proposes

But had it not been for the war it is highly unlikely that Melinda would have married him. He was part of her Paris life, for several months the major part of it; but there are indications that it was a part of her life she would in normal circumstances have been ready to leave behind her when she returned home.

His obvious liking for her was reassuring to Melinda who, for all her popularity, was a little out of her depth. She

was no intellectual and her interest in art and literature was amateurish; on the other hand, politics and economics meant nothing to her.

But she was fascinated by the scope and intensity of the life around her and longed to be able to plunge in and swim with the others. Maclean, who seemed to combine in his tall, handsome person all the qualities which she felt to be lacking in herself, gave her confidence and brought out the latent high qualities which always needed a stimulus.

There is a wide gulf between liking a man's companionship and a desire to marry him.

It was a gulf Melinda did not really contemplate crossing. She indicated as much to her mother — who was also her closest friend. In a letter written soon after she had met him, she said "but I am not really in the least bit interested in him."

That is certainly not convincing evidence, but as time went on she gave no indication that she had changed her mind which, in view of her relationship with her mother, she would have done had she really fallen in love

As it was, it required Hitler's blitzkrieg to bring matters to a head and force Melinda to take one of the two most vital decisions of her life. After she and Maclean had known each other for nearly seven months, the German armies broke into

446

ners
ance

Maginot Line and the war
ily started.

American citizens had already
en advised to return home but
w, with the fighting nearing
is, there could be no
rther delay. And then
lean asked Melinda to marry

he was in an agony of in-
ision. She liked him too well
an outright refusal and yet
could not bring herself to
ept him.

he desperately wanted time.
ld she not go back home and
nk it over? No, he replied.
American citizens could
ain any longer in the war
e and if she went to the
ted States she would never
able to return to Europe—
least, until the war was over.

'No'—then
'Yes'

And as things were then, in
ost the blackest moments of
war, who dare possibly pre-
when that would be, or what
future held?

n her little hotel bedroom
t door to the Café Flore, with
nic rapidly rising all around
Melinda wrestled with her
blem, alone and with no one
guide her. Finally she made
her mind: she could not
rry him.

After another attempt to make
change her mind, he

A mass of contradictions

accepted her decision and said
he would drive her to Bordeaux
and put her on a boat for
America. But events moved too
swiftly for them. The speed of
the German advance accelerated;
the evacuation of Paris began;
and Melinda changed her mind.

On June 10, 1940, with gunfire
sounding faintly in the distance,
Melinda Marling and Donald
Duart Maclean were married in
the Mairie of the Palais Bourbon
district of Paris, facing the
already deserted Chamber of
Deputies

Some time before, in a letter
posted on June 9, although in
typical Melinda fashion it was
dated June 11, she wrote in a
rather extraordinary manner to
her mother, extraordinary, that
is to say, for a young girl just
about to marry the man she
loved. It said:

"Darling Mother,—Please don't
feel hurt that I haven't let you
know before about my decision
to marry Donald. But I honestly
didn't know whether to or not.

"We decided very suddenly
because it seemed to be the only
chance as the Embassy is liable
to have to leave Paris for some
God-forsaken little place in the
country and one is no longer
allowed to travel without an impossible reason.

"Also I had decided I couldn't
stand it any longer I was so
homesick.

"I am sorry I haven't given
you more details about Donald
and I know that you must be very
worried and also probably dis-
appointed at my marrying an
Englishman. But that doesn't
necessarily mean I will have to
settle down in England for the
rest of my life. We will probably
be sent all over the world.

"Darling, I am terribly in love
with Donald and am sure there
will never be anyone else. He
is the only man I have ever seen
I would have liked to marry. We
have known each other nine
months now, so you see we are
not blindly rushing into it

An unreal
world

The letter was obviously continued some days later, by which
time the infuriating French red
tape had been successfully
reduced to mere strings and the
marriage was imminent. Melinda
speaks of a dinner at the home
of a friend of Donald's who had
a car:

"And when they leave Paris
Donald and I are going with him.
I will probably go straight to
Bordeaux to try to get a boat. I
am so thrilled I can hardly
believe I will soon be seeing you.
I am only bringing over two suit-
cases or so as it will be impossible to travel with more. The
rest I am leaving in Donald's flat
as they will be sent to him if he
has to leave France."

The utter unreality of this
letter, written after the German
armies had overrun Europe and
were fast approaching Paris—
facts of which it makes no mention at all—show Melinda's pre-
occupation with her own affairs
to the complete exclusion of the
outside world, a characteristic
which, I think, she always
retained

Plans go
wrong

The letter continued:
"To go back to Donald,
sweetie. He is six foot four,
blond with beautiful blue eyes,
altogether a beautiful man. He
has all the qualities for a husband
(at least, I think) He is the soul
of humour, responsible, a sense of
humour, intelligent, imagination,
cultured, broad-minded (and
sweet), etc.

"Of course, he has faults, but
somenow they don't clash with
mine—except that he is stubborn
and strong-willed I needed that
as I was drifting along getting
nowhere.

"My greatest desire is to have
a baby while I am home as I am
dying to have one and I couldn't
bear to have it without you.
Wouldn't it be wonderful,
Mummy!"

It is clear from this that
Melinda had planned to marry
Donald and then, with his influence and as the wife of a
British official, obtain a passage
to America from Bordeaux or
some southern French port.

447

But things did not work out like that. After their wedding they took to the road in what was in effect a nightmare honeymoon. Paris was emptying fast and the roads leading out of the capital were jammed with refugees. Donald and Melinda, with a friend in whose car they were travelling, got only as far as Chartres and they spent their first married night in a field.

They head west

The next morning they headed west. They were living in a time of the most extraordinary uncertainty and confusion, but they still hoped it would be possible to spend a few days' honeymoon before deciding upon the next move.

They had thought of going to Biarritz and, indeed, after reporting to Bordeaux, where the British Embassy had established itself, they did spend two days in a village not far from Biarritz. But once again events moved ahead of them: the capitulation of France, now led by Marshal Pétain, was imminent and, with it, the evacuation of the British Embassy.

They hurried back to Bordeaux and there, on June 23, they went on board a British destroyer which sailed in the late afternoon. Three hours later, out at sea but still within sight of France, they were transferred to a British tramp steamer, and in it they made a fantastic journey of ten days to England.

[World copyright]

TOMORROW:

● **The diplomatic round: London, Washington, Cairo**

● **Maclean's strange moods**

The woman Melinda

HER voice was slightly husky, slightly breathless, American in timbre, certainly, but the almost accentless voice of the educated, travelled classes.

Her sisters—usually any girl's most candid critics—say that, anyhow, until the birth of her first child, Melinda had an exquisite figure—and indeed when I first met her, when she was 32, she could have changed very little, for she was still extremely attractive.

She dressed in excellent taste but did not appear to be deeply interested in clothes. She had a kind of casual, effortless elegance which could make a battle-dress look smart, and in a way seemed to prefer old clothes to new—a somewhat unusual taste in a woman. Possibly it was that she was so often preoccupied with her own thoughts and dreams—whatever they were.

Her moods

An incident, highly revealing of Melinda's attitude towards clothes, occurred while she and Maclean were living in Washington when he was First Secretary at the British Embassy there and they were invited to what was Melinda's first White House ball.

Her immediate reaction was the entirely feminine one of "I've absolutely nothing to wear." The second step was also normal: frantic telephone messages to her favourite New York store to order a dazzling new creation.

But then came an abrupt departure from the accepted pattern of feminine behaviour. The dress arrived, was tried on, approved—and practically forgotten. Melinda simply could not be bothered with it and went to the ball in a little frock belonging to one of her sisters.

She was always very popular in almost any circle —and yet entirely lacked self-confidence. She was naturally shy yet gregarious as a starling; extremely lazy but given to sudden bursts of energy; vague but capable of decision and determination; vain but curiously humble; apparently frail and defenceless but in fact tough and self-reliant. And although she was generally tractable she could on occasion be quite dominant.

Her weakness

But, unlike Maclean, who was definitely a split personality, one man one day and quite another the next, there were no two Melindas: this was Melinda, this living amalgam of moods and tempers, differing from hour to hour as another facet caught the prevailing influence, but always unmistakably the same girl.

She lived on her emotions, was swayed primarily by her emotions. She had an excellent mind, but was mentally lazy and rarely took the trouble to think things out for herself if she could find someone to do it for her.

It was thus that when, aged 23, she met 26-year-old Donald Maclean she became completely under the influence of his keen, incisive mind and his knowledge of the world—already so much greater than her own.

Imperceptibly, unconsciously even, Melinda began to take her views from him —except possibly on politics, in which she was always utterly without interest—and this, plus her loyalty and, to some extent, her vanity, was her undoing.

[World copyright]

was a Communist., was probably a Communist herself, and
was going off to join him.

Melinda, usually the gentlest

lengthy period of heart-
breaking suspense.

ON MONDAY

*The wedding. Flight through
war-time France. An extraordinary letter*

Only nine weeks

to join a declaration that they
did not know where he was.
At least keep the money and
await developments.

So, with the assistance of an
urbane gentleman from the
Foreign Office, Mrs. Dunbar
opened a special account in a
London bank and deposited in
it the money.

The significance of this relatively large sum of money,
arriving only nine weeks after
a penniless Maclean dis-
appeared, is clearly enormous.

Life in the Foreign Service is
difficult for anyone without
private means and Maclean,
who had none and was not a
provident person, had always

The remainder of the £6,500
purchase price had been
obtained by a mortgage, of
which both interest and capital
repayments had to continue
after Maclean had gone. If he
was no longer providing for his
family, they felt that he had at
least made an effort to repay
part of his financial debt to
Melinda.

Where did Melinda think he
had obtained this sum of

Mr. Tamm
Mr. Sizoo
Mr. Winterrowd
Tele. Room
Mr. Holloman
Miss Gandy

Ten years older

I went down to Beauvallon from Paris at the end of September and persuaded a badly shaken Melinda—who at that time seemed to have aged ten years since I last saw her some months before—to dine with me in St. Tropez.

We left with her mother and sister and brother-in-law in his car without attracting the intention of the amateur sleuths, but, after dinner, as we were strolling along the quay, flash-bulbs exploded as one of the ever-watchful photographers tried unsuccessfully to take our picture.

Melinda and her family were allowed to enjoy the last fortnight of their holiday in peace.

Agonising doubts

The official who came down to Talsfeld in the middle of August questioned Melinda on the most intimate details of her life with Maclean. He suggested...

But Mrs. Dunbar and right insisted that Melinda must get away from Talsfeld for a time. She and her family and their friends had been trying to take Melinda's mind off the tragedy of which she was the central figure, but although Melinda was courageous and sensible, she was by now in desperately poor spiritual and physical shape.

"It was too terrible," she said to me one day. "It was like being suddenly forced to live like some strange, rare fish in an aquarium with everybody looking at me, pointing at me, talking about me."

On balance the holiday was worth while, although during the first fortnight reporters swarmed to Beauvallon.

WHO IS THE MYSTERIOUS MR. BECKER?

The bank were giving nothing away to Mrs. Maclean's mother.

right to go abroad if they wished, that they were permitted to leave. But before they left Melinda had one of her few unpleasant interviews with the security officers in charge of the case.

The senior M.I.5 officer with whom Melinda had had all her dealings, a courteous and intelligent man who, if he had an iron hand, most carefully concealed it inside a velvet glove, telephoned to say that he wanted to talk to her before she left. But later he said he was indisposed with a bad knee and was sending a colleague in his place.

pounds in her purse, with his own account overdrawn to the extent, it is believed, of just over £100, and the usual accumulation of debts.

So far as can be ascertained, the bank has made no efforts to have this overdraft paid off. Certainly it did not approach Melinda for this purpose.

Then, on June 1, 1951, the Foreign Office suspended him for being absent without leave. And from that day his wife received not a penny from her husband's employers—no more salary, no gratuity, no pension. Melinda herself had a small private income, but it was insufficient to keep her and her family — now increased to three.

One reason why Mrs. Dunbar thought the £2,000 from Switzerland had been sent by or for Maclean was that it was the exact sum Melinda had raised on her American securities to make the down payment on Beaconshaw.

A 'loftier note

Two days later the Union Bank of Switzerland also replied in a slightly loftier line. They wrote:

"We do not know Mr. Becker. At the present time we are not in a position to communicate with the above-mentioned gentleman. We must leave it to you to return the said cheek to us."

What was to be done with the money? Mrs. Dunbar and Melinda were all for tearing up the cheques, but a wise official of M.I.5 persuaded them not to.

He pointed out that the money had been sent by Maclean for the use of his wife and children whom he had left, so far as any material support he was able to provide was concerned, practically penniless.

Into the bank

There was, he argued, no evidence at all that Maclean was behind the Iron Curtain

... had failed completely and the bank divulged no additional information of any value. It is, however, probable that they had nothing to add.

The mysterious Mr. Becker, whose real name was certainly something entirely different, would have to do nothing more than walk into the bank, fill in a form requesting that a remittance of £1,000 should be made to Mrs. Dunbar in London, sign it with a name and an address no one would seek or wish to verify, and pay the necessary sum.

Confirmation is to be found in the replies Mrs. Dunbar received to her two letters. On August 22 the Swiss Bank Corporation wrote that the cheque for £1,000 "was ordered at our counter by Mr. Robert Becker. The cheque was paid for in cash by Mr. Becker, who is unknown to us. Nor were any particulars given by him with regard to the remittance."

M.I.5 object to Melinda's holiday in France

by

GEOFFREY

HOARE

ON August 14, 1951, at the suggestion of M.I.5, Mrs. Dunbar (Melinda's mother) wrote to the two banks at St. Gall in the hope—not very rosy—that as the money had been sent to her they might unbend sufficiently to give her a little more information.

She pointed out that she knew no one called Robert Becker (the man in whose name the two £1,000 drafts were sent) and asked if they could give her any further details of the unexpected remittance.

The ruse

been chronically hard-up. His abrupt and unplanned departure from Cairo left his wife more or less stranded there with little money and a lot of bills.

After his sick leave he decided that he did not wish to go abroad again for some years, and accepted a post at the Foreign Office. This meant that he lost nearly all the allowances which make life a little easier for members of the Foreign Service abroad, and he was reduced to his basic salary which, even for the high rank of Counsellor, is only in the region of £1,500 a year—minus income tax.

That was indeed little to maintain a wife and two children in a large house in the country and to enable Maclean to lead the kind of life he was living in the two or three months preceding his dis-

money—more than one year's salary on his Foreign Office scale and yet amassed in some way in only nine weeks?

She refused to believe he was behind the Iron Curtain. The only explanation certain of his friends could think of was the possibility that he had gone off with a wealthy woman who was providing him with money—that he had, in fact, become some kind of a gigolo.

On August 17 Melinda and her three children, her sister Mrs. Terrell and her little boy, and Mrs. Dunbar went to the south of France as they had planned before Maclean dis-

of women, flared up. "You have proved nothing against my husband," she said. "Until you do I'll never believe he was a traitor to his country."

It was on these terms that the interview ended. But when the official had gone Mrs. Dunbar found Melinda in deep distress.

Again she was filled with agonising doubts. Had he really been a Communist all the time? Was that, she asked bleakly, why they had been so unhappy in Washington?

Away from Tatsfield

"Oh, Mummy," she said helplessly. "Maybe you can be married to a man for a long time and really never know him at all."

The Foreign Office, too, had not wanted them to go abroad.

THE MISSING MACLEANS: THIRD INSTALMENT

by order of } Mr. Robert Becker, Hotel Central, Zurich,
and for account of

£ 1,000.-- Cheque No. 060054 on London to your order

A reproduction of the business part of the draft sent to Mrs. Melinda Dunbar from the Swiss Bank Corporation

MYSTERY OF THE £1,000 CHEQUES

by
GEOFFREY HOARE

DURING those June days of 1951 Melinda Maclean waited at Beaconshaw in increasing distress and agony of mind for news of her missing husband. She waited also for the imminent birth of her third baby.

On June 12 her sister Harriet and her husband arrived at Tatsfield and the next day Melinda went into hospital. And there, in the early morning of Thursday, June 14, twenty days after he had deserted her at a time when above all a woman has need of her husband, she wrote a letter to Donald. It was found, still unopened, among the papers she left behind in her Geneva flat after her disappearance in September, 1953.

Melinda and Donald Maclean
These were their happy days

100-374[illegible]
NOT RECORDED
191 SEP 9 1954

53 SEP 1 1954
210

"NEWS CHRONICLE"
London 8-26-54
RE: DONALD D. MacLEAN, ETAL
ESPIONAGE - R

452 5/994

'My dearest'

A previously used white envelope was sealed with a wide band of blue paper on which was written, in pencil, "To Donald Duart Maclean from Melinda Maclean." The letter, also in pencil, said:

My dearest Donald,

If you ever receive this letter it will mean that I shan't be here to tell you how much I love you and how really proud of you I am. My only regret is that perhaps you don't know how I feel about you.

I feel I leave behind and have had a wonderful gift in your love and the existence of Fergie and Donald. I am so looking forward to the new baby. It seems strangely like the first time and I think I shall really enjoy this baby completely. I never forget, darling, that you love me and am living for the moment when we shall all be together again.

All my deepest love and wishes for a happy life for you and the children.—MELINDA.

This letter was written before Melinda drifted slowly away into the anæsthetised sleep from which she might well never emerge, for the birth of her third baby, which, medically, she should not have had, was dangerous in the extreme.

Might expect

It was the letter of a courageous and generous girl, of a girl, moreover, who, despite everything, still loved the man whose child she was about to bear. And, whatever happened afterwards, whatever she may have felt and said from time to time, this letter helps to explain her actions two years later.

But this touching letter had curious omissions. It made no reference of any kind to Maclean's disappearance. Melinda was still taking the attitude that she refused to believe that he was a "traitor" and had gone behind the Iron Curtain, and that is clearly what she believed.

But what did she think had happened to him? One might have expected in this possibly farewell letter there would be reference to the fact that he had left her some such sentence as "wherever you are, whatever you are doing," some expression of her forgiveness for the grievous wrongs he had done her.

On the other hand, if she had any knowledge or even suspicion of what he was doing, where he had gone, one would certainly have expected her to reveal it in a letter which was intended for Donald only if she died.

Why she did not afterwards destroy this letter, why she kept it with her for 27 months and then left it behind, is another mystery.

Money

The baby, a healthy girl, was born during the morning, and although Melinda was extremely ill, she recovered fairly quickly and 14 days later she left hospital to face, again, the tragic difficulties of being the wife of the Missing Diplomat.

By the time she returned to Beaconshaw most of the Press had realised that Melinda and her family knew nothing more about Maclean's disappearance than they read in the newspapers. She had, moreover, been requested by the Foreign Office to say nothing.

In the weeks between the birth of her baby daughter and the time she and her family left England for a holiday in the South of France, Melinda was near to breaking point.

It was towards the end of July that Mrs. Dunbar, who had originally planned to take the two boys to France for a seaside holiday while Melinda had her baby, decided that it was imperative to get Melinda away.

Another daughter, Mrs. Catherine Terrell, went to France and, after consulting estate agents, rented a large,

shabby house called La Sauvageonne, standing in its own grounds at Beauvallon, not far from St. Tropez. Before they could go, two important developments occurred.

On Friday, August 3, five weeks after Melinda and her new baby daughter—also called Melinda—left hospital, Mrs. Dunbar received two registered letters from St. Gall, near Zurich, in Switzerland.

One was from the Swiss Bank Corporation and the other from the Union Bank of Switzerland, and each contained a draft in her name on a London bank for £1,000.

The printed forms accompanying the cheques were almost identical. They stated merely that the remittance was made "by order of Mr. Robert Becker, Hotel Central, Zurich." Mrs Dunbar knew no Robert Becker and was expecting no money from Switzerland.

But it was obvious, anyway, that the money had come, in some way, from Donald Maclean and had been sent to her rather than to Melinda in case the name Maclean, still very much in the news, attracted attention.

Mr. Becker

Mrs. Dunbar immediately rang up M.I.5 and experts hurried down to Tatsfield to examine the letters and take them away for closer inspection.

Detectives flew to St. Gall where, with the help of the Federal Police, they attempted to trace Mr. Becker. They were unsuccessful.

There is nothing in the world "closer" about its affairs and the affairs of its clients than a Swiss bank, and apart from a vague description of the man who had bought two £1,000 cheques and the information that he had indicated that he was staying at the Hotel Central, Zurich, and had given an address in New York, there was nothing else to be discovered.

And even this was little use. No one of that name, it was found, had stayed at the Hotel Central, and as for the New York address, it was non-existent. But, as New York streets are numbered, American detectives were able to state that Mr. Becker's residence, had it existed, would have been approximately in the middle of Central Park.

Then, two days later, Melinda received a letter from Maclean. It was undated and bore no indication of when it had been written, but it had been posted the previous day, August 4, in England—at the main post office at Guildford in Surrey, only about 25 miles from Tatsfield.

Must know

It was in the circumstances a most extraordinary letter, affectionate, loving, the kind of letter a husband, suddenly called away on business might have written to his wife to explain that he was frightfully sorry he had gone off so hurriedly, but would soon be back.

It made no reference to where he was or what he was doing. But it said that she must know in her heart that he had to do what he had done (which meant entirely nothing to Melinda), but that he could still not tell her why he went or where he had gone. He said:

"I don't know what you must have thought of me going off and leaving you with no money."

M.I.5

He stated that he had sent £2,000 to her mother for her and the children: "I thought it would be better that way."

He hoped she and the children were well and as tenderly after the new baby which he knew had been born and was a girl.

It contained a fatuous phrase about "I can imagine you with a daughter," which was not in the least like Maclean, whose ordinary letters were amusing and far more sophisticated than that. And it asked whether the baby was fair like the other children or dark like Melinda. And it ended with his love.

The letter was most carefully examined by officials of M.I.5, who came rushing down to Tatsfield when Melinda phoned to tell them she had received it. The writing was undoubtedly his, but it was a little shaky, a little uncertain.

The phraseology, if a little stilted, was on the whole the kind which he might conceivably have used, but it did not ring quite true, was not quite a natural style.

Melinda felt that it

letter he had written either within dictated limits or which he knew would have to stand scrutiny to see that he was giving nothing away.

The paper was ordinary—it could have been bought anywhere in England or on the Continent. But that was of no importance.

The people who had taken charge of him, who had arranged his flight and who had permitted him to write this belated last letter to the wife he had deserted, were certainly in a position to obtain whatever kind of letterpaper suited their purposes.

Moscow

Had it been the headed notepaper of the Foreign Office, or the House of Commons or of the Athenæum Club, it could still have been written and dispatched in Moscow, to be posted by a Communist agent in Paris, Rome or London.

The only possible points of significance were the reference to the new baby and the information that he had sent Melinda £2,000.

This meant that the letter had been written after June 14 and he was aware that the baby had been born and was a girl, information which could be obtained from the announcements of births in The Times and from the columns of many other newspapers.

The question of the money was interesting in its connection with the timing of the letter. It implied a close liaison between agents in Switzerland and London, although the letter only stated that the money had been sent. It did not necessarily imply that he knew it had been received — which would indeed have been an outstanding feat of espionage.

Melinda

But to Melinda the letter meant two facts of overwhelming importance. Firstly, it was proof that he was still alive and disproof of the theories then being advanced that he was dead, either murdered deliberately by Communist agents or killed accidentally in a brawl. And secondly it told her what in her heart she was so anxious to know—that he still loved her.

The letter, when it was returned to her by M.I.5, became one of her most treasured possessions, to be carried constantly in her handbag where it still reposed on that day two years later when she went off into the unknown to join the man who had written it.

[World copyright]

TOMORROW:

What happens to the £2,000; Melinda decides to holiday in France; M.I.5 call again

454

NOW MELIND

M.I...

by
Geoffrey
Hoare

The first Di
is told: "
husband v

THE story of the flight of Maclean and Burgess to France is the only part of the disappearance of which there is reliable, corroborated evidence.

They left Tatsfield soon after 9 p.m., in the car Burgess had hired in his own name, and drove through the night to Southampton.

That morning also Burgess, again in his own name, had booked two berths on a cross-Channel steamer, the Falaise, which left Southampton at midnight on Friday for a week-end excursion cruise to St. Malo and the Channel Islands, returning to Southampton early on Monday morning.

Drinking beer

They drove up to the docks in Southampton with only a few minutes to spare; so pressed for time were they that Burgess left the car standing on the quay side.

THE START OF THE JOURNEY

A car of the type in which Burgess and Maclean drove to Southampton stands by the Channel steamer Falaise which took them to St. Malo

This attracted the atte of a car-park attendant called out after them as ran towards the boat. B shouted in reply, "Bac Monday"

This incident alone, i ing as it did, the discove the car still standing for in the docks on Monday after the Falaise had be helped to identify the more effectively than have a chance encounter Paris plane.

The Falaise reached St. at 10 a.m. on the Sat morning, but Burgess Maclean remained on drinking beer until the passengers had disemb and they then went a leaving in their cabins th gage they had brought them — Maclean's bri and two suitcases of belonging to Burgess.

They appear deliberat have missed a train tha St. Malo at 11.45 for Par their actions for two me were trying to get away out being seen were fa beyond words.

455

Mr. Harbo...
Mr. Mohr...
Mr. Parsons...
Mr. Rosen...
Mr. Tamm...
Mr. Sz...
Mr. Winterrowd...
...le Room
...Hullman
...ndy

I SEES MAN

pearance—and she n't worry,' your be, back soon"

An urgent signal

They were reported as ...ving gone first into a café ...d then an hotel to try to ...hange English money, and ...hen to have hired a taxi to ...rive them to Rennes, fifty ...iles away, where they could ...atch the train they missed at ...t. Malo.

There is certainly no evi-...ence that they did in fact ...oard the train, and while the ...tory of the taxi journey was ...learly related in good faith ...y the driver, the French Sûreté were by no means satis-...fied of its reliability.

"The identification appeared to be open to doubt," they told me.

From that moment the two men disappeared utterly and completely.

The remarkable difference between the amateurishness of the first part of the disappear-...ance and the efficiency of the second stage is one of the most curious aspects of the whole mystery.

At Tatsfield, the morning after they left, the guests arrived and Melinda had to explain to them that Maclean had been unexpectedly called away—as she watched the drive with ever - increasing anxiety for his return.

On Sunday, May 27, Mrs. Dunbar — Mrs. Maclean's mother—by chance telephoned from Paris to ask after the health of the two little boys, who were ill with measles.

Melinda said to her in a low, miserable voice: "Oh, Mummy, I wish you would come over. I'm afraid Donald has gone off on a drinking party again."

On the Monday morning, still without news of him, Melinda telephoned to his office and was told that he had not arrived.

And that afternoon she again telephoned, but this time to speak to Mr. G. A. Carey-Foster, the Foreign Office's Chief Security Officer. She told him that Maclean had gone away for the week-end with a friend named Roger Styles but had not returned.

Mr. Carey-Foster was re-...assuring. "Don't worry," he said, "I'm sure, your husband will be back soon. But I think it would be best if you said nothing at all about this to any-one else."

Clearly, however, a more serious view was taken when the Chief Security Officer reported Donald Maclean's "non-appearance." High-level inquiries were immediately opened.

That night an urgent signal was sent out to all British diplomatic and consular posts on the Continent to look out for Maclean and his companion and report back on a "clear-the-line" level to the Prime Minister. In other words, the message was to have the high-est possible priority and was to be sent in plain language to avoid any delay in coding and decoding.

Guy was missed

At the same time the various special branches, M.I.5 in England, M.I.6 and other agencies abroad were alerted, but no warning was sent to the French or other European police.

At this stage the Foreign Office obviously hoped it would be possible to find Donald Maclean and his companion without any publicity.

When did the Foreign Office know that Maclean's com-panion was not an unknown Roger Styles but Guy Burgess, very much known in official circles ?

Burgess's mother, Mrs. Bassett, telephoned to the Foreign Office either on the Monday or the Tuesday to say that her son was missing. His disappearance h a d been noticed, despite the errant bohemianism of his usual life, because he had not kept two highly important engagements.

And the captain of the Falaise h a d notified his superiors that two passengers had failed to rejoin the ship when she left St. Malo.

Mrs. Dunbar arrived from Paris on Wednesday, May 30, in response to her daughter's telephone appeal. She found Melinda, who in any case was far from well, extremely worried and upset, but by no means overcome by grief, for at that time she clearly ex-pected Donald to return.

It leaks out

He had been gone five days, and although that was a long time indeed for a drunken escapade—which was the ex-planation which Melinda was clinging to—it did not seem to her entirely outside his extra-ordinary capacities.

It was on that day, in the London apartment of Lady Maclean, Donald's mother, that Melinda first met the senior M.I.5 officer who was in charge of the investigations. He was brought there by Mr. Carey-Foster and not to Beaconshaw, because Melinda had to be in London to see her doctor.

The interview that day was short and matter-of-fact. The investigators seemed at that time also to expect Donald to return—at least, that was the impression they gave Melinda.

But it is now clear that by May 30 the authorities must have been in possession of a good deal of information, cer-tainly that Maclean's com-panion was Burgess and that they had gone to France. Obviously t o o, whatever Melinda may have believed, the authorities did not place much reliance in the early theory of a hectic week-end in Paris.

Obviously it was necessary sooner or later to seek the co-operation of the French police. When was this done ?

The impression I gained in Paris at the time was that the French police were not in-formed of the disappearance until some six or seven days after it was discovered.

Mr. Herbert Morrison later suggested that the co-operation of the French police had been requested only one day after the disappearance had become known.

Once the French police knew, a "leak" was inevitable and the only surprising thing is that it was so slow in arriving.

On Wednesday, June 6, an inspector at the Sûreté Nationale told a French jour-nalist, who worked also as an informant for an English news-paper, that they were looking far two missing British diplo-mats. That was sufficient.

456

The Paris correspondent telephoned to his London office. Inquiries were made, and the next morning the news was blazoned across the front page of two British newspapers.

When Melinda read the headlines, "Two British Diplomats Missing," and the story below which suggested that they were "trying to get to Moscow," she said pathetically to Mrs. Dunbar, "Oh, Mummy, they can't be referring to Donald, can they?"

Wire from France

Her fears that the headlines pointed at Donald were confirmed the next morning. Not only were the names Donald Maclean and Guy Burgess impossible to avoid whenever one looked at a newspaper, but telegrams from the missing men were received that day.

There were two from Donald: one to his mother, Lady Maclean, signed by his childhood nickname "Teento," and the other to Melinda.

They had been posted in the Post Office in the Place de la Bourse in Paris, which is open all night for telegrams, at 10 p.m. the previous day by a heavily made-up woman. The original of the telegram received by Melinda contained many mistakes in English, most of which were corrected in transmission. It read:

MRS. MACLEAN MELINDA. BEACON SHAW. TATSFIELD NEAR WESTERHAM. SURREY. ENGLAND. HAD TO LEAVE UNEXPECTEDLY. TERRIBLY SORRY. AM QUITE WELL NOW. DON'T WORRY DARLING. I LOVE YOU. PLEASE DON'T STOP LOVING ME. DONALD.

Two-fold search

This was both meaningless and frightening. The foreign handwriting and the obvious mistakes showed that Maclean could not have written it. That meant either that he had had an accident or that he was no longer a free agent.

But even if he had dictated it, he would at least have got the address right. He would not have placed Tatsfield in Surrey when he knew that its postal address was Westerham, Kent.

And, anyhow, the whole message rang false. It was not a telegram he would ever have sent. "Am quite well now": he had not been ill when he left. "Don't worry, darling"; what insufferable futility!

This t e l e g r a m, to be paralleled 27 months later after Melinda, in her turn, had disappeared, throws an interesting light on the mentality of the organisers of these disappearances.

The two-fold search for the two men—unofficial and highly publicised by the Press: official and shrouded in complete secrecy, by the security organisations — reached its zenith during the next few days.

While hordes of zealous reporters besieged Tatsfield, scores of their colleagues scoured the Continent. A few more details were added to the insignificant little mound of known facts—and a massive mountain of conjecture, speculation and rumour soared every day higher and higher.

A string of questions

What the police and the Intelligence services discovered was not revealed, and if the Government knew anything they kept it to themselves.

Sniped at angrily by a Press which felt itself baulked of official confirmation of its various theories about the Missing Diplomats and their fate, the Foreign Secretary, Mr. Herbert Morrison, was finally forced to make a statement in the House of Commons on June 11. For any light it threw on the mystery he might just as well have saved himself the trouble.

His statement ended with the words: "The security aspects of the case are under investigation and it is not in the public interest to disclose them."

A few more facts, more interesting than anything contained in the original statement, were elicited by a string of questions. The most important and the most reassuring, was the Foreign Secretary's assertion that there was no evidence that Maclean and Burgess had taken documents with them.

But in reporting the debate the next day one newspaper noted that. Mr. Morrison "appeared evasive" when asked whether they possessed any knowledge which had potential value to Russia.

It was, anyway, a fairly difficult question to answer. Who could know what these two men knew? Had they really been collecting information for Russia—of which there was no evidence at all—they could easily have gone outside their own particular niches in the Foreign Office.

Mr. Morrison was at pains to decry the importance of Donald Maclean's position as Head of the American Department — which Mr. Eden described as "perhaps the heaviest and most onerous position in the Foreign Office at the present time "—by pointing out that many of the "matters concerned with negotiations with the United States are actually dealt with in other departments."

A Foreign Office spokesman followed this up the next day. He said that the American Department was not responsible for current questions such as North Atlantic Treaty Organisation matters: the Japanese Peace Treaty or problems considered by the United Nations Atomic Energy Commission.

All they said

In fact, he said, it rea concerned itself with "domes developments i n s i d e United States and questions purely Anglo-American c cern."—whatever that mi mean.

What were extremely teresting in the Commons bate were the tributes to Don Maclean. Mr. Morrison, a stating that the medi evidence was that Macle had fully recovered from breakdown, said that "a rep on Mr Maclean's work v that he was an exceedin able official."

Then came Mr. Antho Eden, who had been Fore Secretary when Maclean v at the British Embassy Cairo.

"May I be allowed to say Mr. Maclean was serv under me at the time in Eg that all the reports I recei of the work he did there w very good indeed ?"

And to this day, that really the sum total of all "official sources"—the Fore Office and the Governmen had to say about the appearance of Maclean Burgess. There have b other statements, many them—all equally negative. equally unilluminating.

[World copyright]

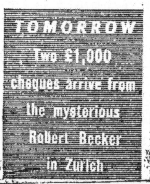

TOMORROW

Two £1,000 cheques arrive from the mysterious Robert Becker in Zurich

457

Mr. Nichols _____
Mr. Belmont _____
Mr. Harbo _____
Mr. Mohr _____
Mr. Parsons _____
Mr. Rosen _____
Mr. Tamm _____
Mr. Sizoo _____
Mr. Winterrowd _____
Tele. Room _____
Mr. Holloman _____
Miss Gandy _____

ANS: First article in the
ells THE WHOLE STORY

FFREY HOARE
tory of Donald
e diplomat who
in 1951 with Guy
' of his wife who
vith their three
st year. World
reserved in all
articles

IY BURGESS

AN BETWEEN

DONALD MACLEAN

458

THE MISSING MA

exclusive series th

Toda
begi
Mac
disa
Bur
van
chil
copy

MELINDA MACLEA

459

SHE BEGGED HIM NOT TO GO WITH BURGESS

IT was a smiling May evening in 1951 when this story that was to echo round the world began in a large house at Tatsfield, near Westerham, in Kent. It was the home of the Macleans.

Donald Maclean, then aged 37 and a promising senior official in the Foreign Service, had for six months been head of the American Department of the Foreign Office.

This appointment followed sick leave of six months while he was recovering from a "nervous breakdown" which developed while he was serving as Counsellor and Head of Chancery in the British Embassy at Cairo.

He was living with Melinda and their two children, Fergus, aged seven, and Donald, five, at Beaconshaw, their rather isolated house at Tatsfield.

CLUB LIFE
Then no news

For a few months after he had resumed work at the Foreign Office at the beginning of November, Donald Maclean had led a fairly regular life, catching an early train back to Tatsfield each evening and spending his spare time with Melinda and the children.

In April this placid domesticity came to an end, and he reverted gradually to the Maclean of earlier days in their married life, going from office to bars and clubs in the West End instead of going home.

About this time, too, he began spending nights in town and once or twice Melinda was without news of him for two or three days at a time.

This is important in view of the circumstances of his disappearance. The change in his behaviour coincided with the return to England of a friend who had visited him in Cairo.

DISGRACE
For Burgess

Guy Burgess had been sent back from Washington, where he had been Second Secretary at the British Embassy, in considerable disgrace. He was on the point of forestalling possible dismissal from the Foreign Service by resigning, and was considering an offer of a well-paid post on a London newspaper.

Since his return to England on May 7 he had been living in London, renewing old friendships in a succession of luncheon, dinner and drinking parties.

There is no evidence, however, that his meetings with Donald Maclean were more than casual, even accidental; they were not close friends.

Mrs. Maclean was expecting her third baby and as the birth, like that of her two previous children, was to be a difficult Cæsarean, the date was known well in advance; it was to be June 14.

HAPPY
But not long

Her mother, Mrs. Dunbar—who arrived in Cairo on a previously planned visit to Melinda just after Maclean's precipitate return to London had left her in financial difficulties and in a state of considerable anxiety—had gone back to the United States in November.

Mrs. Dunbar had promised to come to England about a fortnight before Melinda's baby was born, and then, while Melinda was recuperating, take the two small boys to France for a holiday. There they would be joined by their parents in August, when Maclean's leave was due.

Melinda had passed an extremely busy and, in many ways, happy winter getting Beaconshaw into some sort of shape. Her furniture had arrived from Washington and from Cairo, and she was endlessly occupied in making curtains, doing odd painting jobs and making the neglected house into a home.

From just before Christmas, 1950, until the following spring was one of the happiest times in her life.

But this was not to last. By the middle of May, when Mrs. Dunbar arrived back in Paris to stay there with her youngest daughter Harriet, Maclean's erratic behaviour was again casting shadows over Melinda's life.

46

For some days before May 24 Maclean had been asking Melinda - when her mother would arrive — an inquiry which later became significant.

On Thursday, May 24, the day before his thirty-eighth birthday, Donald told Melinda that a friend of his named Roger Styles—of whom she had not previously heard—would be coming down to dinner the next evening.

Melinda was annoyed. Her baby was only three weeks ahead. She was feeling wretched and in no condition to entertain, especially someone she did not know.

Her small boys had measles, and even in ordinary circumstances, with only one daily servant who went home at tea-time, Beaconshaw was not an easy house to run. It was a relic of the opulent pre-war days when servants were easy to get.

In addition, Maclean's sister Nancy and her American husband and Mrs. Mary Maclean, widow of an elder brother who was killed in the war, were to spend the week-end with them. It was for this reason that Maclean had taken the Saturday morning off.

There was nothing to be done but to accept the unwanted guest with good grace, and the next morning Melinda baked Maclean a birthday cake and prepared a special dinner.

THE HOUSE AT TATSFIELD

Beaconshaw, the house where the strange events occurred. Standing on the lawn is Fergus, the elder son of Donald and Melinda Maclean

So far as can be discovered, Donald Maclean not only spent the Friday—until the evening —in a normal manner, except possibly that his luncheon was more elaborate and prolonged than usual, but his manner was entirely normal.

He caught his usual train, the 5.19 from Victoria to Oxted, and arrived home at the usual time—usual, that is to say, for those evenings when he went straight home from the office.

Before his guest arrived he said to Melinda: "After dinner Roger and I have to go out to see someone on business. I'm going to take a few things in case we have to spend the night."

Not unreasonably, Melinda was extremely upset. She followed him into his dressing room, where he went to pack his pyjamas and shaving gear in a brief-case, and they argued.

It was too bad that he had invited an unknown friend for a birthday dinner which she had been foolishly hoping to spend alone with him. But it was intolerable if he and his friend were then going to leave her alone at home for the evening.

And he was not even sure that he would spend the night at Beaconshaw. His relatives were arriving the next morning. Did he realise there would be a great deal of work to be done which she could not manage alone?

WHY?
A child asks

Putting up beds in the guest rooms? Looking after the central heating? All the other household jobs? For they were his small share in helping to run the house.

Melinda begged him not to go. He said that he had to. And Melinda stormed out of the room and went downstairs.

Then occurred a pathetic little incident which only came out two years later—when young Fergus told his grandmother.

His father's and mother's voices raised in argument had wakened the little boy, who slept in an adjoining room, and after his mother had gone downstairs, he got out of his bed and went in to see his father.

"Why are you going away, Daddy?" he asked. "Can I stand at the window and watch you go?" They were the last words he spoke to his father for at least two years and four months.

Maclean replied, "You get back into your bed, you little scamp. I'm not going far; I shall be back soon."

This conversation fixed itself imperishably on the seven-year-old boy's memory — for, despite his promise, his father did not "come back soon."

And then, half an hour later, Guy Burgess arrived at Beaconshaw in a car he had hired in the morning in his own name. Maclean introduced him to Melinda as Roger Styles.

She found him charming and easy to talk to. He seems to have gone out of his way to be pleasant to her and she was definitely attracted by him.

So far as she could judge, and it must be remembered that she had never met him before, his manner was perfectly normal.

There was certainly no obvious constraint. He appeared neither worried nor ill at ease. Neither he nor Maclean that evening gave the impression of a man on the brink of deserting his family, his friends, his country and his very way of life, probably for ever.

There is one curious point. Going over the events of that never-to-be-forgotten evening, Melinda said afterwards that she had a vague feeling, based on nothing she could remember or fix positively, that Donald and Burgess had in fact travelled down from London together. Had they done so it is not easy to see why they pretended to have come separately.

It might be that after dropping Maclean—either at the station, where he would have picked up his own car, or else near Beaconshaw—Burgess had driven off to see someone who lived near.

Dinner was a normal meal with three civilised people talking casually and amicably with no apparent signs of the mental turmoil through which two of them must surely have been passing. There was certainly no hint that evening of the catastrophic storm which was

...soon to break over, those three lives.

After dinner Maclean said, casually, that he and Roger had to go out to see someone on business. They would probably not be long, but Melinda was not to be worried if they were late.

Melinda, in the presence of the guest, asked merely whether the "business" could not possibly be put off until the morning, but he said, regretfully, that it could not.

He then went out into the garden to make up the furnace for the central heating, a job Melinda in her condition could not do. While he was away Melinda and Burgess talked idly, and again Melinda was struck by his charm.

FAREWELL
His words

Maclean returned, and then, with some remark about not being long—there was no further reference to the possibility of being away for the night—they went.

And that was Melinda's farewell to her husband, and, for all its petty annoyances and disappointments, one of the most peaceful days she was to have for many months.

She read for a time and then, as there was no sign of his return and she was very tired, she went to bed early.

This series is from a book to be published by Messrs. Cassells.

TOMORROW

- *The flight to France. Melinda receives the guests, tries to explain Maclean's absence*
- *She says to her mother on the 'phone: 'I'm afraid Donald has gone on a drinking party again'*
- *She tells the Foreign Office. Enter M.I.5*
- *The news breaks. The search begins*

462

THE MISSING M
WERE MY FR

by Geoffrey Hoare

No other writer is better suited to tell the story of the Missing Macleans. First, he was their friend. He knew them long before their names were printed across the pages of the world's Press. Then, as Paris Correspondent of the News Chronicle, he reported the disappearance of Maclean and, last year, of Melinda and the children.

He is a friend of Mrs. Maclean's mother, Mrs. Dunbar. And, so that a true picture might be given, she provided him with fresh facts, letters and photographs. With this background and his own knowledge of the affair, Hoare has written a book as fascinating as it is important.

From that book the News Chronicle has taken the series of articles which begins tomorrow. Today Geoffrey Hoare tells how and why he wrote it.

Melinda Maclean w
Deauville, i

463

CLEANS
NDS

Hoare on the beach at Villers-sur-mer, near
. The next summer she disappeared

I HAVE been more deeply interested in the mystery of the Missing Diplomats than most people, and in a somewhat better position to try to penetrate it. For one of them, Donald Maclean, and his wife Melinda were my friends.

They had been my neighbours in Cairo. From there, indeed, Donald and I had flown back to England together on the completion—although neither of us then knew it—of our respective terms of service in that part of the world.

Decision

After his disappearance I remained in close touch with Melinda during the first two unhappy years of her existence as the Wife of the Missing Diplomat, and it was only in the final four months before she disappeared that I ceased to hear from her.

After she had gone I became the confidant and friend of her grief - stricken mother, Mrs. Dunbar.

And it was one night last December, in the course of one of our endless discussions of this tragedy which had fallen on her and her family, that I decided with her approval to write "The Missing Macleans," a book which would try to present a true picture.

The Case of the Missing Diplomats. Donald Maclean and Guy Burgess, was one of the major sensations of 1951. For the world at large it opened on Thursday, June 7.

SENSATION

ON that pleasant summer morning, when the Korean war was barely a year old, the story of these two men first broke on an England which at first hardly realised its importance.

The headlines were bold and black, but the stories beneath them were guarded. And there was no mention of the two names which were to become a byword of the times we live in. Said one report:

Scotland Yard officers and French detectives are hunting for two British Government employees believed to have left London with the intention of getting to Moscow.

A friend is quoted as saying they planned the journey for their idealistic purposes.

The two men are employed by the Foreign Office and there is a possibility they might have important papers with them.

Several experts have flown from London to France to work with the French police, and all French airports and frontiers are being watched. The police, it is understood, are watching visitors to the Soviet Embassy in Paris.

No newspaper sensation could have had a better beginning. The story had all the ingredients — missing diplomats, flight to Moscow, important papers, airports and frontiers watched, Soviet Embassy involved.

That same afternoon the Foreign Office—a week late—reluctantly divulged sufficient details to give the brew more body.

An announcement from Whitehall said that two members of the Foreign Service had been missing from their homes since May 25. They were Mr. D. D. Maclean and Mr. G. de M. Burgess.

All possible inquiries are being made. It is known that they went to France a few days ago. Mr. Maclean had a breakdown a year ago owing to overstrain but was believed fully to have recovered.

Owing to their absence without leave, both have been suspended with effect from June 1

Since that day, over three years ago, more has probably been published about the Maclean and Burgess mystery in the world's newspapers and magazines than on any other single topic.

Some of it has been the result of painstaking, conscientious investigation, soberly and accurately presented. A lot has been mere sensational reporting. Too much has been unabashed, third-rate fiction.

Certainly the story has never been either easy or straightforward to report. After the laboriously assembled details of the actual flight from England to France, reporters had nothing to go on, for, despite an enormous hue and cry in England and on the Continent, the two men were never seen again.

464

New facts

There the mystery stood until September, 1953, when Mrs Melinda Maclean, Donald Maclean's American-born wife, and her three young children, who had gone to live in Geneva, also disappeared.

Similar intense investigations were undertaken—with almost equally negative results. This time, however, the trail was traced to the borders of the Soviet Zone of Austria.

After several months of work I uncovered many new facts throwing light on how, where and why the Missing Diplomats disappeared, and many clues from which reasonable deductions might be made.

And it is, I feel, a vital story; an important story, as well as a fascinating human story. · ·

SENTIMENT?

AT first I concentrated on Donald Maclean.

What was it that caused him to desert his wife and children, his home, his job—that enviable job in the Foreign Service which held so brilliant a future —his country, and his very way of life?

Could the reason be sentimental—after all, a king did renounce his throne for love? Was it financial? Was he in trouble, threatened with exposure and disgrace?

The answer lies elsewhere. Through the ages men have died for their beliefs. Some still do. But others caught up in the modern clash of conflicting ideologies take the easy way out. They change camps.

And that is what Donald Maclean did, and with him Guy Burgess. They fled their country and went behind the Iron Curtain for the same reasons that impelled Petrov to flee from the Soviet Embassy at Canberra and which sent Dr. Otto John across the frontier to East Germany.

The same reasons which led Nunn May and Fuchs to remain in England and become traitors there.

All these men—and probably others, too—men in good official positions, intelligent, trusted, thoughtful, had listened to the siren voice of propagandists.

Weaklings

They had come to distrust the way of life in their own countries and imagined, in the case of Burgess and Maclean, that only on the other side of the Curtain were security and sanity to be found.

But they were weaklings, with grievous faults in their make-up which made them terribly vulnerable and, instead of staying where they were and fighting for their beliefs, they fled.

The case of Melinda Maclean is quite different. And in attempting to unravel her role in this mystery, I have traced her life from childhood through marriage to her last agonising days in the free world.

This investigation, which entailed talking to her friends and relatives and reading the letters she exchanged with her husband and her family, was an essential task in trying to find a clue to a mystery even deeper than that posed by Donald Maclean's own disappearance.

Why did Melinda, the deserted wife who was on the point of remaking her shattered life, suddenly follow him into exile?

She had no ideological convictions. She was not interested in international politics or world affairs. She was an attractive, uncomplex person, a normal wife and mother. And yet she went—taking her three small children with her.

TRAGEDY

IT was only by a close examination of the personalities and actions of these two unhappy human beings that a possible answer could be found. And it was in an attempt to provide that answer, and to try to clear away the misunderstandings, the exaggerations and the misrepresentations which have always clouded this modern tragedy, that I wrote this book.

THE LAST PICTURE TOGETHER

It was taken in the garden of Beaconshaw at Tatsfield just before Maclean disappeared. Melinda Maclean was then expecting her third baby

TOMORROW: The story begins

The quarrel over Burgess; Maclean insists on bringing him home for dinner; the disappearance.

465

Tolson _____
Boardman _____
Nichols _____
Belmont _____
Glavin _____
Harbo _____
Rosen _____
Tamm _____
Tracy _____
Mohr _____
Wintercrowd _____
Tele. Room _____
Holloman _____
Miss Gandy _____

DELETED COPY SENT (B. MacDonald
BY LETTER 9 SEP 22 1976
PER FOIA REQUEST

Mrs. MacLean Wrote Mother In 1953 After She Vanished

LONDON, Aug. 19 (P).—The American-born wife of vanished British Diplomat Donald MacLean has sent word in a mysterious letter postmarked Cairo that she and her husband are "well and happy," the Foreign Office confirmed today.

The letter was written by Mrs. Melinda MacLean, 38, to her mother, Mrs. Melinda Dunbar, who showed it to British Foreign Office officials. The Foreign Office said the letter was dated October 24, 1953, but declined comment on the delay in releasing news of it.

MacLean vanished May 25, 1951, with fellow Diplomat Guy Burgess and it was believed they fled behind the Iron Curtain. His wife disappeared with her three children in Switzerland last September, apparently to follow her husband into exile.

Although the letter bore an Egyptian postmark, officials emphasized it could not be assumed Mrs. MacLean mailed the letter in Cairo herself.

"It could have been taken to Cairo in a diplomatic pouch," an official said. "There are many possibilities."

MacLean served in Cairo before becoming chief of the North American section of the Foreign Office in London. Just a month before he vanished, he suffered a breakdown at his Cairo post.

First word of the letter appeared in the London press to-day, attributed to "informed sources." The newspaper reports apparently smoked out the Foreign Office on the latest chapter in the mystery that has perplexed the West.

MRS. DONALD MacLEAN
... writes to mother.

100-37183

76 AU 25 1954

11 AUG 26 1954

Wash. Post and
Times Herald
Wash. News
Wash. Star
N. Y. Herald Tribune
N. Y. Mirror
Date: 8-20-54

XI

Mr. Tolson
Mr. Boardman
Mr. Nichols
Mr. Belmont
Mr. Harbo
Mr. Mohr
Mr. Parsons
Mr. Rosen
Mr. Tamm
Mr. Sizoo
Mr. Winterrowd
Tele. Room
Mr. Holloman
Miss Gandy

MACLEAN MYSTERY UNFOLDS

Melinda—'I could not have done otherwise'

THE FULL AND AUTHENTIC STORY STARTS NEXT WEEK

RE: DONALD DUART MACLEAN, ET AL
ESPIONAGE - R

NEWS CHRONICLE
AUGUST 20, 1954
LONDON, ENGLAND

OFFICE OF THE LEGAL ATTACHE
AMERICAN EMBASSY
LONDON, ENGLAND

DELETED COPY SENT C.B. MacDonald
BY LETTER JUN 22 1976
PER FOIA REQUEST jwg

NOT RECORDED
191 SEP 9 1954

100-3??1?

467

THE News Chronicle yesterday broke the long silence that has blanketed the world mystery of the Missing Macleans.

This newspaper announced that the first FULL and AUTHENTIC story of the missing diplomat, Donald Maclean, and his wife, Melinda, who vanished last year with her three children, will begin in this paper next week.

The announcement rocked the rest of Fleet Street. Rival newspapers, realising with commendable celerity its significance and the widespread national concern in the Maclean and Burgess affair, groped for any particle of news, however slender, in their efforts to catch up.

Particularly they grasped at the disclosure that Mrs. Maclean wrote to her mother, Mrs. Dunbar, after she disappeared last autumn.

Bold headlines were flung urgently across front pages: MRS. MACLEAN WRITES TO MOTHER; MRS. MACLEAN WRITES HOME; A LETTER FROM MRS. MACLEAN.

But their accounts showed that Fleet Street's news editors still do not know what lies behind this most extraordinary mystery.

LETTER FROM CAIRO

Today the FACTS about the letter can be carried a stage further. Facsimile extracts from it are reproduced on this page. The letter was posted last October in Cairo—not from "somewhere in Eastern Europe."

It was short and infinitely pathetic. It opened: "Darling Mummy," and said "they" were well. She hoped "with all my heart" that her mother would understand how deeply she felt the "sorrow and worry" her departure would cause.

It said they all missed Mrs. Dunbar and asked her to believe that "in my heart I could not have done otherwise than I have done."

The letter—it was written on a single sheet of grey-blue notepaper—forms only one episode in the story of the Missing Macleans and of Donald's diplomat friend Guy Burgess, who accompanied him on his journey into the unknown. There is much more to tell.

IT WILL GRIP EVERYONE

The whole narrative, related by Geoffrey Hoare, Paris correspondent of the News Chronicle, is one that will grip every reader.

Fleet Street wants to know the facts.

You want to know the facts.

These facts will be given in Hoare's exclusive series of articles starting next week in the NEWS CHRONICLE.

It is the *full* story. It is the *true* story. It will be widely read not only for its human interest but for its national importance.

It contains some of the most significant revelations ever printed of this strange age in which we live.

There will be a tremendous demand for the NEWS CHRONICLE from Monday onwards and you will be well advised to make sure of reading the Missing Macleans by placing an order with your newsagent now.

468

Darling Mummy
I know you will
be worrying terribly
but please believe
me that we are all
quite alright

MELINDA'S LETTER HOME

Darling Mummy, I know you will be worrying terribly but please believe
me that we are all quite alright

Goodbye but not
for ever —
Melinda

THE LAST WORDS SHE SENT

Goodbye but not for ever—Melinda

469

Mme M. H. Dunbar
7 Avenue de Segur
Paris VII ème
France

THE CAIRO ENVELOPE
Postmark, October 24, was six weeks after Mrs. Maclean and the children vanished from Switzerland

470

Mr. Tolson
Mr. Boardman
Mr. Nichols
Mr. Belmont
Mr. Harbo
Mr. Mohr
Mr. Parsons
Mr. Rosen
Mr. Tamm
Mr. Sizoo
Mr. Winterrowd
Tele. Room
Mr. Holloman
Miss Gandy

DELETED COPY SENT   C.B MacDonald
BY LETTER JUN 22 1970
PER FOIA REQUEST

(JOHN)
BERLIN--THE WEST BERLIN NEWSPAPER BX REPORTED WEST GERMANY'S MISSING SECURITY CHIEF, OTTO JOHN, WAS A FRIEND AND ACCOMPLICE OF GUY F. BURGESS, ONE OF BRITAIN'S "MISSING DIPLOMATS."
BX SAID BURGESS HELPED JOHN ESCAPE TO LONDON WHEN HE FLED FROM GERMANY IN 1944, AND THAT JOHN RETURNED THE FAVOR BY HELPING TO SMUGGLE BURGESS AND DONALD D. MACLEAN THROUGH THE IRON CURTAIN IN 1951.
THE REPORT WAS THE LATEST OF A SERIES OF RUMORS SET OFF BY JOHN'S DISAPPEARANCE INTO SOVIET BERLIN LAST WEEK. THE COMMUNISTS--AND JOHN HIMSELF, IN A SERIES OF RECORDED PROPAGANDA STATEMENTS--SAY HE WENT VOLUNTARILY, BUT WESTERN OFFICIALS BELIEVE HE WAS LURED OVER THE BORDER.
INTELLIGENCE SOURCES SAID ANNEMARIE WEYRES, NURSE-RECEPTIONIST EMPLOYED BY DR. WOLFGANG WOHLGEMUTH, HAS DENIED REPORTS THE DOCTOR DRUGGED JOHN BEFORE THEY LEFT TOGETHER FOR THE COMMUNIST SECTOR.
THESE SOURCES SAID MISS WEYRES, WHO HAD BEEN MISSING SINCE JULY 20 WAS "LOCATED AND INTERROGATED," APPARENTLY IN FRANKFURT.
7/30--MJ&GE1011A

100- 304183

471

SEP 10 1954

NOT RECORDED
191 SEP 9 1954

WASHINGTON CITY NEWS SERVICE

0-20

Mr. Tolson _____
Mr. Boardman _____
Mr. Nichols _____
Mr. Belmont _____
Mr. Glavin _____
Mr. Harbo _____
Mr. Rosen _____
Mr. Tamm _____
Mr. Tracy _____
Mr. Mohr _____
Mr. Winterrowd _____
Tele. Room _____
Mr. Holloman _____
Miss Gandy _____

(PETROV)
LONDON--A GOVERNMENT MINISTER CONFIRMED REPORTS THAT VLADIMIR PETROV, SOVIET DIPLOMAT WHO SOUGHT ASYLUM IN AUSTRALIA HAD PROVIDED INFORMATION ABOUT TWO BRITISH DIPLOMATS WHO DISAPPEARED IN 1951.
MINISTER OF STATE SELWYN LLOYD TOLD COMMONS UNDER QUESTIONING THAT PETROV HAD TALKED ABOUT GUY BURGESS AND DONALD MACLEAN. THEY WERE RUMORED TO HAVE GONE EASTWARD THROUGH THE IRON CURTAIN, BUT NO OFFICIAL WORD OF THEIR WHEREABOUTS EVER WAS FORTHCOMING.
ASKED HOW MUCH PETROV WAS TELLING ABOUT BURGESS AND MACLEAN, LLOYD REPLIED:
"WE ARE IN CLOSE TOUCH WITH THE AUSTRALIAN GOVERNMENT, WHO HAVE APPOINTED A ROYAL COMMISSION TO INVESTIGATE THE CASE OF MR. PETROV. THE INTERROGATION IS AT PRESENT IN PROGRESS.
"BUT SUCH INFORMATION ABOUT BURGESS AND MACLEAN WHICH HAS SO FAR BEEN ELICTED IS OF A LIMITED AND GENERAL CHARACTER, AND IT IS NOT YET CERTAIN WHETHER IT IS BASED ON PETROV'S PERSONAL KNOWLEDGE OR HEARSAY."
5/3--WO641P

DELETED COPY SENT   C. B. Mac Donald
BY LETTER JUN 22 1970
PER FOIA REQUEST

100-374183

5 0 MAY 17 1954

472

191 MAY 14

| Mr. Tolson |
| Mr. Boardman |
| Mr. Nichols |
| Mr. Belmont |
| Mr. Glavin |
| Mr. Harbo |
| Mr. Rosen |
| Mr. Tamm |
| Mr. Tracy |
| Mr. Mohr |
| Mr. Winterrowd |
| Tele. Room |
| Mr. Holloman |
| Miss Gandy |

More than 4,000,000
sale every day

OPINION

THE FOREIGN OFFICE OBJECTS...

INTENSE and voluble activity in the Foreign Office! With what object? To discredit, as far as possible, a sensational report in the Daily Express from its crime reporter, Percy Hoskins.

Hoskins said that Vladimir Petrov, ex-agent of the Russian secret police, has told Australian security officers how the missing British diplomats Burgess and Maclean escaped, where they are at present, and what they are doing.

The Foreign Office replies that Petrov had only hearsay knowledge of the Burgess - Maclean affair, and no detailed information. Later it admits that Petrov has indeed given information about them.

Really, gentlemen!

THE Foreign Office is wasting its time and ours.

Is it seriously suggested that a key Russian agent in a key centre of the Russian spy network (Australia) could fail to glean an immense amount of information about Burgess and Maclean?

"DAILY EXPRESS"
London 4-29-54

Let common sense prevail, whether in chairs at the Foreign Office or in more comfortable seats elsewhere.

It gets around

BURGESS and Maclean represent one of the great triumphs of the organisation to which Petrov belonged. Inevitably, many details about that triumph have passed from one Russian agent to another—even as far as Canberra, where Petrov had been three months when Burgess and Maclean disappeared.

Whether the details Petrov has passed on are the truth or not, the Daily Express does not know. Does the Foreign Office know?

The one certainty is that Petrov *can* tell the truth, or a good deal of it.

Answer this charge

HOWEVER, before the Foreign Office pours its next elegant sprinkling of not-too-cold water on the Petrov story let it pause to read the front page of the Daily Express this morning.

There Chapman Pincher says that the Foreign Office had been warned by M.I.5, months before Maclean fled, that Maclean was unreliable politically and unstable emotionally. Yet the Foreign Office, while acting on a similar report about Burgess, shelved this one on Maclean.

A grave charge is made. Is Chapman Pincher's story true? If so, which officials in the Foreign Office read M.I.5's devastating report? And on what grounds did they take the responsibility for ignoring it?

Questions that demand immediate reply. ——

DELETED COPY SENT   C.B. MacDonald
BY LETTER
PER FOIA REQUEST

1/60
NOT RECORDED
191 MAR. 14 1954

100-3/4183

Feb
5
69

473

53 MAY 17 1954

Petrov confirms it

Maclean working behind Curtain

Express Political Correspondent

A FOREIGN OFFICE spokesman said yesterday that Vladimir Petrov has no "first-hand knowledge" of the missing diplomats Burgess and Maclean. But I can reveal that he has given information confirming that they are behind the Iron Curtain.

The Foreign Office said that "hearsay" evidence given by Petrov, former Russian diplomat, about Burgess and Maclean "must be treated with some reserve."

But last night's spokesman agreed that Petrov, who is in political asylum in Australia, HAS been questioned about the missing diplomats, and that early reports on the interrogation HAVE reached London, as stated in the Daily Express yesterday.

The report in the Daily Express said that the material supplied by Petrov about Burgess and Maclean and other episodes of post-war disappearances and kidnapping will need several months of checking and rechecking.

The Daily Express did NOT state that Petrov had "first-hand knowledge" of the missing

→ PAGE TWO. COL. FOUR

"DAILY EXPRESS"
London 4-29-54

PETROV CONFIRMS IT

FROM PAGE ONE

diplomats; but that, as head of the Russian secret activity in Australia, he had access to files showing the escape route followed by the two men and a list of agents who helped them in their defection.

As the Foreign Office so energetically put forward yesterday, a full account has not yet been received from Australia of the evidence which has been given by Petrov."

And, as the Daily Express indicated, couriers with more and more of Petrov's disclosures are arriving at centres of Western Intelligence.

Chapman Pincher writes: It was revealed yesterday that months before Maclean and Burgess fled the country in May 1951 the Foreign Office had been warned that both men were unfit for positions of trust.

A report on Maclean was made by M.I.5 agents, who shadowed him during 1950 while he was taking six months' "sick leave" following an outburst in Cairo, where he broke a colleague's leg by wildly swinging a rifle.

This report clearly stated that the security authorities were satisfied that Maclean was unreliable politically and unstable emotionally.

A similar report on Burgess followed his return from the post of second secretary at Washington in May 1951.

The Foreign Office chiefs acted on the report on Burgess—but shelved the warning about Maclean.

Instead of dismissing Maclean they appointed him head of the American division—although he was openly disagreeing with the foreign policy of the Western allies.

Six months later he disappeared with Burgess behind the Iron Curtain at a time when the resumption of the Anglo-American partnership on atomic weapons was being considered.

Mr. Tolson
Mr. Boardman
Mr. Nichols
Mr. Belmont
Mr. Glavin
Mr. Harbo
Mr. Rosen
Mr. Tamm
Mr. Tracy
Mr. Mohr
Mr. Winterrowd
Tele. Room
Mr. Holloman
Miss Gandy

DELETED COPY SENT   C. B. MacDonald
BY LETTER JUN 22 1976
PER FOIA REQUEST

100-374783

474

Mr. Nichols ....
Mr. Belmont ....
Mr. Glavin ....
Mr. Harbo ....
Mr. Rosen ....
Mr. Tamm ....
Mr. Tracy ....
Mr. Mohr ....
Mr. Winterrowd ..
Tele Room ....

MACLEAN: PETROV TELLS

THE FULL STORY OF VANISHED DIPLOMATS SENT TO BRITAIN

MACLEAN

BURGESS

The Red spy system has crumbled

Express Crime Reporter PERCY HOSKINS

AS a result of disclosures made by fast-talking Vladimir Petrov, ALL is now clear to British Intelligence about the missing diplomats Burgess and Maclean.

Petrov, former third secretary at the Russian Embassy in Canberra, has revealed the WHEREABOUTS of the diplomats ; HOW they are employed ; HOW they are paid.

He has told Australian Security officers the names of those WHO planned the escape route which Burgess and Maclean took nearly three years ago.

Petrov, former chief in Australia of the Russian secret police, has also told WHO helped the diplomats to get across the Continent.

And heavily guarded couriers are daily bringing to London these secrets and others concerning disappearances and kidnappings to behind the Iron Curtain.

"DAILY EXPRESS"
London 4-28-54

C.B MacDonald

LETTER JUN 1957
PER FOIA REQUEST

NOT RECORDED
191 MAY 18 1954

5 2 MAY 19 1954

475

WIFE IS TALKING TOO

With Petrov is his 35-year-old honey-blonde wife Evdokia. She was a cypher clerk in the embassy—and she was, it is further revealed, a key operative in the secret police.

With her husband—in political asylum in a hiding place in New South Wales—she is talking fast too.

Couriers are bringing copies of their statements by plane not only to London but to the Intelligence Departments of the other Western Powers.

Revealed already are the details of most Communist subversive activity in the West since 1945, when Igor Gouzenko, Russian cypher clerk in Ottawa, exposed the spy rings in Canada.

The leak of Communist spy activities has become a waterfall—so that all branches of the Intelligence Services of NATO are now fully occupied checking facts, identifying agents, and tracing payments to "fifth columnist" co-operators.

And this work will go on for months—while the Communist spy organisation will plainly have to be overhauled.

MOSCOW REORGANISES

Old agents will no longer carry trust; and, if still free, they will have to be recalled. All their contacts will be under observation. And fresh agents will find the going tough.

Already, yesterday came news of developments in Moscow, where Prime Minister Malenkov has reorganised his Government.

And the most notable change is the setting up of a State Security Committee, independent of Sergei Kruglov, the Minister of the Interior who succeeded Beria, the shot "traitor."

To the head of this new committee goes General Ivan Serov, until now deputy to Kruglov. He becomes the supreme boss of Russia's espionage, counter-espionage, and sabotage activities.

And Serov, 48-year-old ladies' man and favourite of Stalin, with a long record of undercover arrests in Russia, will have the task of reorganising his foreign services—in the light of Petrov's revelations.

It is not yet known how much of Petrov's disclosures will be made public. Some will certainly be aired before the Royal Commission of Investigation which is being set up in Australia.

NOW MPs MAY BE TOLD

In Britain, the Foreign Office will decide how far the freshly gained details of Burgess and Maclean will be made available through Parliament.

Donald Maclean, immaculate but erratic, was the 38-year-old head of the American Department in the Foreign Office. Guy Burgess, shiftless and erratic, was 40, and had been second secretary at Washington.

They caught the steamer Falaise at Southampton on May 25, 1951, landed at St. Malo, took a taxi to Rennes, in Brittany—and vanished from the eyes of the Western world.

Since then there have been two indications that Maclean is alive—(1) An emissary placed £1,000 in a Swiss bank for the benefit of his dependants; and (2) Mrs. Maclean and her children vanished eastwards from Geneva last September.

And there has been one indication that Burgess is alive—he sent Christmas greetings to his mother, in Arlington House, S.W., last year.

The Petrov story, when it can be told in full, will complete the Burgess and Maclean story—the most baffling in the history of British Intelligence.

[World Copyright Reserved]

HE IS TALKING —FAST

VLADIMIR PETROV
His secrets flown to London

476

Tolson _____
Ladd _____
Nichols _____
Belmont _____
Clegg _____
Glavin _____
Harbo _____
Rosen _____
Tracy _____
Mohr _____
Trotter _____
Winterrowd _____
Tele. Room _____
Holloman _____
Miss Gandy _____

WHY DON'T THE BRITISH QUESTION HIM?

Ex-Spy Boasts He Was Reason Burgess Went Behind Curtain

By SEFTON DELMER London Express Staff Writer

DUSSELDORF, Germany—You would expect that British Intelligence officers would at least give a routine check-over to a man who:

● Is a close friend of Guy Burgess, the vanished British diplomat;

● Has himself fled from Britain to the Iron Curtain and holds a job now in a communist office in Berlin's Soviet sector;

● Is an ex-Briton;

● Is an ex-diplomat;

● Is at present visiting his mother in West Germany and therefore available for questioning?

But so far no British Intelligence officer has bothered 52-year-old Baron Wolfgang zu Putlitz in his Cologne hotel. Only Dr. Otto John, head of the German Security Services, has had a chat with him.

WILLING TO TALK

The baron is quite ready to chat. "You know," he said, "I may have been the indirect inspiration of Guy Burgess's decision to come over to us." He smiled and added: "Of course I cannot be certain that Maclean and Burgess are with us. I have never seen them or even been told anything about them. But then—such things are secret.

"However, I have a good notion that I was responsible. Yes, that is possible—very possible."

And he smiled again.

FOUGHT HITLER

Wolfgang zu Putlitz, member of a Junkers family, had used his position in the German Foreign Office to fight Hitler by passing secret information to the British between 1935 and 1939.

But in September 1939 he managed to get on a plane and escaped from The Hague to London.

"Burgess," said the baron, "had been an intimate friend of mine since 1934. He was immensely impressed with what I had done. He kept telling everyone we met he thought I was the bravest man he had ever met."

Last time Putlitz and Burgess met

GUY BURGESS

was at the farewell party Burgess gave in his Bond-st. flat before his departure for America.

Putlitz, a naturalized British citizen by then, was given a $20-a-week job as a shipping clerk in London.

"I could hardly live on that," he said. "I had to eat fried fish every day. My rent alone cost me $12 a week.

"But while I starved Britain began to support the rearmament of Germany and the rebirth of German militarism.

"Everything in fact was being restored that I abhorred and to fight which I had sacrificed my name and my career.

"I decided to get out and go over to the Russians." He travelled secretly to Berlin, crossed into the Russian zone, surrendered his British passport to the German communist police, who gave

him an Eastern zone passport in its place.

Then he joined a communist publishing firm.

By now the baron was well launched on the propaganda line he had come to the West to preach:

● How the Soviet Union's only policy with regard to Germany was Germany's demilitarisation and de-Nazification.

● How the German People's Police Army had been formed in Eastern Germany purely as an answer to West German rearmament. They would be disbanded at once, he said, if the West abandoned rearmament.

● How the Russians themselves were longing to leave Germany if only the other occupying Powers would do the same.

● How the reunion of Germany could be quite simply effected by talks between the West Germans and the East Germans themselves without interference from the allies.

● How they hoped to make a little extra money by arranging for some West-East business deals.

Certainly the baron looked as though he could do with some cash. His face looked drawn and worn and far older than when I had last seen him in London almost nine years ago.

"But," and up flashed the propaganda line, "I am happy to be fighting Nazism again."

Well, there it is. Don't you think this friend of Burgess is a man our Intelligence experts should take the trouble to look over while he is around?

Wash. News
Wash. Star
81 APR 9 1954 N.Y. Herald Tribune
100-37/183 N.Y. Mirror

NOT RECORDED

Date: 3/25/54

APR 12 1954

DELETED COPY... C. B. MacDonald
BY LTR... JUN 22 1976
PER FOIA REQUEST

| Mr. Tolson |
| Mr. Boardman |
| Mr. Nichols |
| Mr. Belmont |
| Mr. Glavin |
| Mr. Harbo |
| Mr. Rosen |
| Mr. Tamm |
| Mr. Laughlin |
| Mr. Mohr |
| Mr. Winterrowd |
| Tele. Room |
| Mr. Holloman |
| Miss Gandy |

Ex-Communist Reveals To 'The Yard' Trail Through France Was False—They

HOW BURGESS AND MACLEAN DID IT

DELETED COPY SENT ____ C.B. MacDonald
BY LETT... JUN 22 1976
PER FOI... REQUEST

OFFICE OF THE LEGAL ATTACHE
AMERICAN EMBASSY
LONDON, ENGLAND

NOT RECORDED
46 APR 9 1954

"SUNDAY DISPATCH"
London 3-21-54

Re: Guy Burgess, etal
Espionage - R
5 2 APR 13 1954

478

Fled In Plane, He Says

By JAMES REID, Sunday Dispatch Crime Reporter

SCOTLAND YARD Special Branch have been told how missing diplomats Guy Burgess and Donald Maclean flew out of Britain as V.I.P.s while accomplices laid a false trail by another route.

This new information was given to politicians by a one-time top-ranking British Communist who recently broke away from his party.

A senior official of the Labour Party drafted a full report last week and sent it to Commander Leonard Burt of the Special Branch.

Agent At The Airport

This is the ex-Communist's story:

Burgess and Maclean did not leave England by cross-Channel steamer as has been understood. Their departure was planned months in advance by international Communist agents who left false trails to suggest that the two men had reached the Continent by way of Southampton and St. Malo—thereafter travelling to Paris.

Instead, says the informant, the two travelled out of Britain by air.

They were passed through the airport as V.I.P.s, with the connivance of a Communist agent who "eased" their departure so that attention was not drawn to them, and no record left of the fact that they passed that way.

They flew to Düsseldorf. At the airport there they were met by a Communist agent and lived for several days at his home to avoid police attention. Afterwards they flew again. They are said now to be in Prague.

Doubles Were Used

The informant said that this method of departure has been carried out successfully on other occasions. He told [...] officials that it has been made easy because of [...]

appeared in May 1951. For months the Secret Service tried to check their movements, without success, though it has always been believed they went over to the Communists and may be working on their behalf behind the Iron Curtain.

One theory is that they are helping Russia in her diplomatic dealings with the West.

For a time Maclean's American-born wife, Melinda, lived at their home in Surrey. Then she went to Switzerland with their three children.

Mrs. Maclean and her children disappeared from Geneva last autumn and it is thought they have joined Maclean and are living at the village of Kladno, 15 miles from Prague.

This story has not been accepted unreservedly by the authorities. But because of the high position held by the informant in the Communist Party it is being given serious thought.

[World copyright reserved.]

479

Fled In Plane, He Says

By JAMES REID, Sunday Dispatch Crime Reporter

SCOTLAND YARD Special Branch have been told how missing diplomats Guy Burgess and Donald Maclean flew out of Britain as V.I.P.s while accomplices laid a false trail by another route.

This new information was given to politicians by a one-time top-ranking British Communist who recently broke away from his party.

A senior official of the Labour Party drafted a full report last week and sent it to Commander Leonard Burt of the Special Branch.

Agent At The Airport

This is the ex-Communist's story:

Burgess and Maclean did not leave England by cross-Channel steamer as has been understood. Their departure was planned months in advance by international Communist agents who left false trails to suggest that the two men had reached the Continent by way of Southampton and St. Malo—thereafter travelling to Paris.

Instead, says the informant, the two travelled out of Britain by air

They were passed through the airport as V.I.P.s, with the connivance of a Communist agent who "eased" their departure so that attention was not drawn to them, and no record left of the fact that they passed that way.

They flew to Düsseldorf. At the airport there they were met by a Communist agent and lived for several days at his home to avoid police attention. Afterwards they flew again. They are said now to be in Prague.

Doubles Were Used

The informant said that this method of departure has been carried out successfully on other occasions. He told Labour Party officials that it has been made easy because of the presence of Communists and Red sympathisers at British and Continental airports.

He added that the two men who travelled out of this country via Southampton and St. Malo under the guise of Burgess and Maclean, were doubles and that luggage left aboard the steamer Falaise was a red herring.

The name of the airline official alleged to have assisted the bogus V.I.P.s has been given to the Special Branch.

Maclean and Burgess, both Foreign Office officials, dis-

appeared in May 1951. For months the Secret Service tried to check their movements, without success, though it has always been believed they went over to the Communists and may be working on their behalf behind the Iron Curtain.

One theory is that they are helping Russia in her diplomatic dealings with the West.

For a time Maclean's American-born wife, Melinda, lived at their home in Surrey. Then she went to Switzerland with their three children.

Mrs. Maclean and her children disappeared from Geneva last autumn and it is thought they have joined Maclean and are living at the village of Kladno, 15 miles from Prague.

This story has not been accepted unreservedly by the authorities. But because of the high position held by the informant in the Communist Party is being given serious thought.

[World copyright reserved.]

| Mr. Tolson |
| Mr. Boardman |
| Mr. Nichols |
| Mr. Belmont |
| Mr. Clavin |
| Mr. Harbo |
| Mr. Rosen |
| Mr. Tamm |
| Mr. Tracy |
| Mr. Mohr |
| Mr. Winterrowd |
| Tele. Room |
| Mr. Holloman |
| Miss Gandy |

An ex-spy tells me about BURGESS

DUSSELDORF, Sunday.

YOU would expect, would you not, that British Intelligence officers would at least give a routine check-over to a man who—

ONE: is a close friend of Guy Burgess, the vanished British diplomat;

SEFTON DELMER

puts a man who fled to the Reds on his NEWSMAP

TWO: has himself fled from Britain to the Iron Curtain and holds a job now in a Communist office in Berlin's Soviet sector;

THREE: is an ex-Briton;

FOUR: is an ex-diplomat;

FIVE: is at present visiting his mother in West Germany and therefore available for questioning?

But so far no British Intelligence officer has bothered 52-year-old Baron Wolfgang zu Putlitz in his Cologne hotel. Only Dr. Otto John, head of the German Security Services, has had a chat with him.

The baron is quite ready to chat. "You know," he said to me pensively, sipping his Moselle, "I may have been the indirect inspiration of Guy Burgess's decision to come over to us." He smiled and quickly added: "Of course I cannot be certain that Maclean and Burgess are with us. I have never seen them or even been told anything about them. But then—such things are secret.

"However, I have a good notion that I was responsible. Yes, that is possible — very possible."

And he smiled again.

After listening to his story, I agree. I too think it is very possible."

Escape

WOLFGANG ZU PUTLITZ, member of a Junkers family, had used his position in the German Foreign Office to fight Hitler by passing secret information to the British between 1935 and 1939.

But in September 1939 he managed to get on a plane and escaped from The Hague to London.

"Burgess," said the baron, "had been an intimate friend of mine since 1934. He was immensely impressed with what I had done. He kept telling everyone we met he thought I was the bravest man he had ever met. It was most embarrassing. Probably he made up his mind to follow my example."

Last time Putlitz and Burgess met was at the farewell party Burgess gave in his Bond-street flat before his departure for America.

"It was a terribly wild evening," said Putlitz. "But everyone was there. Even Guy Liddle and Blunt of M.I.5."

Putlitz, a naturalised British citizen by then, was given a £5-a-week job as a shipping clerk in London.

"I could hardly live on that," he said. "I had to eat fried fish every day. My rent alone cost me £3 a week.

"But while I starved Britain began to support the rearmament of Germany and the rebirth of German militarism.

"Everything in fact was being restored that I abhorred and to fight which I had sacrificed my name and my career.

"I decided to get out and go over to the Russians." He travelled secretly to Berlin, crossed into the Russian zone, surrendered his British passport to the German Communist police, who gave him an Eastern zone passport in its place.

Then he joined a Communist publishing firm, where his next-door neighbour is John Peet, the former British Reuter's reporter who also crossed over to the Russians.

His preaching

BY now the baron was well launched on the propaganda line he had come to the West to preach:—

HOW the Soviet Union's only policy with regard to Germany was Germany's demilitarisation and de-Nazification.

HOW the German People's Police Army had been formed in Eastern Germany purely as an answer to West German rearmament. They would be disbanded at once, he said, if the West abandoned rearmament.

HOW the Russians themselves were longing to leave Germany if only the other occupying Powers would do the same.

HOW the reunion of Germany could be quite simply effected by talks between the West Germans and the East Germans themselves without interference from the allies.

HOW they hoped to make a little extra money by arranging for some West-East business deals.

Shabby...

CERTAINLY the baron looked as though he could do with some cash. His face looked drawn and worn and far older than when I had last seen him in London almost nine years ago.

"But," and up flashed the propaganda line, "I am happy to be fighting Nazism again."

Well, there it is. Don't you think this friend of Burgess is a man our Intelligence experts should take the trouble to look over while he is around?

"DAILY EXPRESS"
London 3-15-54

RE: GUY BURGESS, ET AL
ESPIONAGE - R

Mr. Tolson ___
Mr. Ladd ___
Mr. Nichols ___
Mr. Belmont ___
Mr. Clegg ___
Mr. Glavin ___
Mr. Harbo ___
Mr. Rosen ___
Mr. Tracy ___
Mr. Mohr ___
Mr. Trotter ___
Mr. Winterrowd ___
Tele. Room ___
Mr. Holloman ___
Miss Gandy ___

BERLIN--THE WEST BERLIN TELEGRAF REPORTED THAT GUY BURGESS AND DONALD MACLEAN, BRITAIN'S "MISSING DIPLOMATS," ARE LIVING IN RED PRAGUE IN A RESIDENTIAL AREA RESERVED FOR GOVERNMENT OFFICIALS.

THE NEWSPAPER QUOTED UNIDENTIFIED "EASTERN NEWSMEN" AS THE SOURCE OF THE REPORT. 2/18--CE944A

C.B. MacDonald

100-374183

191 FEB 25 1954

WASHINGTON CITY NEWS SERVICE

482

58 FEB 26 1954

Mr. Tolson	
Mr. Ladd	
Mr. Nichols	
Mr. Belmont	
Mr. Clegg	
Mr. Glavin	
Mr. Harbo	
Mr. Rosen	
Mr. Tracy	
Mr. Mohr	
Mr. Trotter	
Mr. Winterrowd	
Tele. Room	
Mr. Holloman	
Miss Gandy	

Two decoys in escape of Mrs Maclean

SWISS POLICE GIVE UP THE HUNT

From Daily Mail Correspondent

ZURICH, Sunday.

SWISS police security chiefs have decided "to drop for the present" further inquiries into the disappearance of Mrs. Melinda Maclean and her three children from Geneva last September.

The decision was taken at a meeting at which they considered every scrap of information they had collected during their five months' investigations.

Interrogations of persons who claimed to have seen Mrs. Maclean and her children travelling by train on the day of her disappearance have led security chiefs to conclude that there were at least two decoys.

"DAILY MAIL"
London 2-8-54

Re: Donald Duart MacLean
Espionage - R

DELETED COPY SENT C.B. MacDonald
BY LETTER JUN 22 1976
PER FOIA REQUEST

100 - 374183

NOT RECORDED
191 FEB 25 1954

OFFICE OF THE LEGAL ATTACHE
AMERICAN EMBASSY
LONDON, ENGLAND
58 FEB 26 1954

483

Mr. Tolson
Mr. Ladd
Mr. Nichols
Mr. Belmont
Mr. Clegg
Mr. Glavin
Mr. Harbo
Mr. Rosen
Mr. Tracy
Mr. Mohr
Mr. Trotter
Mr. Winterrowd
Tele. Room
Mr. Holloman
Miss Gandy

BURGESS AND MACLEAN
Investigations Continuing

Asked by Mr. LIPTON (Soc. Brix ton) for further information about the disappearance of the diplomats Burgess and Maclean, Mr. Selwyn LLOYD stated: "Investigations are still continuing and no detailed account of their nature can be given without prejudicing the chances of their success." Since the letter in Burgess's handwriting received by his mother on Dec. 22, no more definite information had been forthcoming.

When Mr LIPTON pressed for more information. Mr. LLOYD said "If he was to presume they are behind the Iron Curtain he would probably be right."

DELETED COPY SENT O.B. MacDonald
BY LETTER JUN 2 2 1975
PER FOIA REQUEST

NOT RECORDED
191 FEB 25 1954

100-374133

484

"DAILY TELEGRAPH & MORNING POST"
London 1-26-54

Re: DONALD DUART MacLEAN, ET AL
ESPIONAGE - R

OFFICE OF THE LEGAL ATTACHE
53 FEB 26 1954 /AMERICAN EMBASSY
LONDON, ENGLAND

Mr. Tolson _____
Mr. Boardman _____
Mr. Nichols _____
Mr. Belmont _____
Mr. Glavin _____
Mr. Harbo _____
Mr. Rosen _____
Mr. Tamm _____
Mr. Tracy _____
Mr. Mohr _____
Mr. Winterrowd _____
Tele. Room _____
Mr. Holloman _____
Miss Gandy _____

In the footprints of Maclean and Burgess

FOLLOW THE TRAIL WITH THE EXPRESS

The snapshot 'Maclean' left behind him

☆ *Donald Maclean and Guy Burgess, two Foreign Office experts, disappeared together in May 1951 by the simple method of catching a cross-Channel steamer. So started the most amazing hunt of our time, traced and explained in this startling new series.*

WITHIN a few hours of the publication by the Daily Express of the news that two British diplomats had disappeared the House of Commons heard the sensational report confirmed by the then Prime Minister, Mr. Attlee.

Characteristically, the Daily Express and its reporter were snubbed—as if in some way they had erred by doing their duty.

The Government spokesman ignored the obvious fact that by trying to hold such vital information secret the authorities had made it easier for the two fleeing men, and those behind them, to carry out their escape plan.

The French police were the first to point this out to me. I spent the afternoon with one of France's leading investigators.

"Confidentially," he said to me, "do you really think the British want to find these two men?" I could hardly understand the question.

"This puzzles me," said the French detective. "First, why did they delay informing us for three critical days—ample time to organise a hiding-place and an air-flight from France?

"Second, why did they omit vital information—photographs and background—which is always regarded as routine in these cases?"

"Daily Express"
London 12-29-53

Re: Guy Burgess, et al
    Espionage - R

OFFICE OF THE LEGAL ATTACHE
AMERICAN EMBASSY
LONDON, ENGLAND

DELETED COPY SENT C.B. MacDonald 100 - 374183
BY LETTER JUN 22 1973
PER FOIA REQUEST

NOT RECORDED
191 MAR 31 1954

70 APR 1 1954

"*Third*, why did they keep the information from the Press? If they had wished they could have had an immediate alert throughout Western Europe, and that—at least would have hindered any Communist escape plan."

"I suppose the answer to your questions is that the British authorities were not certain that the men had in fact escaped," I replied.

"I do not believe that," said the Frenchman. "Even the most naïve policeman would at least have suspected an accident, and this case is not being handled by the most naïve policeman."

"What do you suggest?" I asked.

"I'm not in a position to suggest anything," he said. "But I know that in common larceny if the thief can get into the house and out of the house while there are people inside we always have the suspicion that it's an inside job."

"You are jumping at conclusions," I said. "What reason have you to think that the two men were being watched?"

"Apparently they thought they were under suspicion. Their getaway has the appearance of a very hurried job."

ESCAPE ROUTE

IN the next few days the British and French investigators on the spot pieced together the escape route which was publicised to the world—the excursion ship, the taxi to the station at Rennes, the train to Paris and then nothing.

I received the impression that the chief investigators did not seriously believe in this route. From what I have learned since I am convinced that Burgess and Maclean never were on the train to Paris, but that *someone* who was in on the escape plot did travel on that train in order to throw a false scent.

One clumsy misstep by that agent persuades me that he was an amateur, called in as an accessory at the last moment.

His mistake, which has not hitherto been divulged, was to leave a snapshot, as if by accident, of Mrs. Melinda Maclean on the seat of his carriage.

THE QUESTION

APPARENTLY he intended this to establish without doubt that the two men had taken the train.

This snapshot, retrieved by the train conductor, was only discovered in the train refuse days later and convinced at least one key investigator that the escape route of the two diplomats led not through Paris but to one of the abandoned airstrips not far from Rennes. A fleeing man, with Maclean's reputation for meticulous detail, does not carelessly leave his wife's photo behind as a guide to his train.

It was therefore necessary to

S. L. SOLON

—the man who first broke the news of the vanishing diplomats in 1951 — writes the second instalment of his Secret History of the hunt for the two men.

weigh the question: If the escape seemed a hasty, nearly bungled job (an inquisitive Customs official might have been an embarrassment), why did the two men have to leave in such a hurry? Who alerted them and for what reason?

The answer is that American F.B.I. men had arrived in Britain in April 1951 and were in consultation with the British authorities on problems of mutual security.

While fully protected by diplomatic immunity Maclean's contacts in Washington and New York had nevertheless aroused suspicions and these were communicated to the British.

HIS FRIENDS

ONE of Maclean's associates was said to be William Remington, now serving a prison sentence for perjury before a Congressional Committee.

Years before, while at the British Embassy in Cairo, Maclean had been known for his caustic anti-Americanism. While this was considered as no more than vigorous frankness by an allied diplomat, it was noticed that Maclean's mood became bitter following an incident involving an American girl.

After an all-night drinking party, Maclean was charged with injuring the girl, and but for the intercession of American friends this incident might have ended Maclean's career.

Maclean, brilliant and personable, had friends in high places in both Washington and London. It is no exaggeration to say that among the British he was regarded by the Americans as the best informed on Anglo-American policy.

By his British colleagues he was regarded as the best

MRS. MACLEAN
As she was two years ago.

equipped to deal with the Americans on issues where differences had arisen.

Did one of Maclean's friends tell him, at the crucial moment, that he was suspect?

The facts are that enough was known about Maclean's Communist leanings by April 1951 to arouse the gravest doubts about his loyalty. His superiors did not take the obvious step to ensure that he would be available for the inquiry that had been requested.

What makes the situation even more amazing is that had Burgess and Maclean failed to keep their rendezvous with their Communist guides in France they could have returned to Britain with a "missed-boat" story and none would have been the wiser.

Behind this apparent ineptitude there seems to be something more deliberate and more sinister. Burgess and Maclean are irretrievably behind the Iron Curtain serving their Communist masters. But where is the man, or the men, who helped the two diplomats to escape?

WORLD COPYRIGHT RESERVED

NEXT: The secrets they possessed . . .

486

Mr. Tolson_____
Mr. Boardman_____
Mr. Nichols_____
Mr. Belmont_____
Mr. Glavin_____
Mr. Harbo_____
Mr. Parsons_____
Mr. Tamm_____
Mr. Tracy_____
Mr. Mohr_____
Mr. Winterrowd_____
Tele. Room_____
Mr. Holloman_____
Miss Gandy_____

Comment

TUESDAY, DEC. 29, 1953.

BURGESS : A SUGGESTION

GUY BURGESS, one of the "missing diplomats," writes to his mother for Christmas. So the whole intriguing, never-ending mystery boils up again.

Wild stories and hair-raising theories are circulated. One American newspaper even links MACLEAN and BURGESS with the missing scientist PONTECORVO, and then with the explosion of the Russian H-bomb.

Such sensational theorising does not sweeten Anglo-American relations, nor help British prestige. If fruitless speculation can be ended by authentic news, now is the time to issue it.

The trouble is that nobody (except, perhaps, a limited official circle) knows anything whatever about the motives or the whereabouts of the two missing men.

Since that day in May 1951 when they were last seen walking from a taxicab to the railway station in Rennes, France, nothing has been known of their movements.

Mystery

THERE were telegrams home, though not in the men's handwriting. There was a draft for £1,000 received by MRS. MACLEAN through a Swiss bank. There was her own disappearance. Now comes the Burgess letter. The rest is silence.

Let us try to get the thing in perspective. MACLEAN and BURGESS were not prominent figures, nor had they great secrets to impart. What knowledge they had must have diminished in value so rapidly that today it would be worthless.

It is their disappearance and the manner of it which gave them importance. To call them world figures is no exaggeration now.

Another point to remember is that they have committed no crime. The police are therefore not officially interested in them except as "missing persons," and have no reason to pursue them or even to make inquiries.

Possibility

THIS does not apply to the security officers of the Foreign Office. They are, of course, very much interested in the case and have kept it open for more than 2½ years.

They must have considered several possibilities. One is that the two men were kidnapped and bundled behind the Iron Curtain. Such disappearances are not unknown nowadays.

But this theory is hardly borne out by the facts of MACLEAN's and BURGESS's departure, nor by the careful arrangements made by MRS. MACLEAN before she too was swallowed up.

It is still likely that they are in Soviet or satellite territory—and if that is so it can only be because they were invited there and were in possession of papers issued by the Soviet authorities.

Security

IF they are behind the Curtain it should not be beyond the resources of our Security organisations to discover it. And if they are not, the task should be even easier.

Strangers cannot appear in any place and settle down without people talking—especially when the strangers are MACLEAN and BURGESS, about whom the world is speculating. People talk even behind the Curtain—behind their hands. It is this sort of talk which Security exists to pick up.

In other words, it is not reasonable to suppose that after 2½ years of inquiries our officers, however baffled in some respects, have drawn a total blank.

We suggest therefore that to clear the air an official statement should be issued providing all the information which it is in the national interest to give.

"DAILY MAIL"
London 12-29-53

Re: Guy Burgess, et al
Espionage - R

DELETED COPY SENT   C.B. MacDonald
BY LETTER JUN 22 1956
PER FOIA REQUEST   JJ 100-374783

NOT RECORDED
191 MAR 22 1954

6 - MAR 24 1954   OFFICE OF THE LEGAL ATTACHE
AMERICAN EMBASSY
LONDON, ENGLAND

487

Mr. Tolson _____
Mr. Boardman _____
Mr. Nichols _____
Mr. Belmont _____
Mr. Glavin _____
Mr. Harbo _____
Mr. Rosen _____
Mr. Tamm _____
Mr. Tracy _____
Mr. Mohr _____
Mr. Winterrowd _____
Tele. Room _____
Mr. Holloman _____
Miss Gandy _____

Was this the Red reward for an H-bomb?

Express Staff Reporter

WHY has Russia apparently changed her attitude towards the missing British diplomats Guy Burgess and Donald Maclean?

For two and a half years after their disappearance there was silence. A silence broken only by Soviet denials that the two men were in Russia.

Then three months ago Maclean's wife, Mrs. Melinda Maclean, and their three children were allowed to join him. Mrs. Maclean caught the night express from Lausanne to Zurich and Vienna on September 11 and vanished behind the Iron Curtain.

And last week came the Christmas greetings letter from Burgess to his mother's flat at Arlington House, S.W.1.

'DIPLOMATIC'

was the letter posted in London, S.E.1, but which British security men are certain was brought in by an Iron Curtain courier under the immunity of a diplomatic bag.

It is also believed that Burgess wrote the letter to his mother, whom he adored, because his resolve weakened when he saw the Macleans re-united.

Why, then, does Russia allow all this after two and a half years of silence and mystery?

Here is one theory advanced by the responsible American news magazine World :—

The flight of Mrs. Melinda Maclean to join her husband was linked with the explosion of Russia's first hydrogen bomb and the work done for the Russians by Harwell's runaway atom scientist Bruno Pontecorvo.

It was part of Pontecorvo's reward from the Russians that he should be allowed to arrange the reunion of his old friends the Maclean family.

The magazine, in putting forward this theory, points out that the careers of the two friends, scientist Pontecorvo and diplomat Maclean, had run strangely parallel from their first meeting in Paris in 1938.

THE DATES

That friendship grew while they were both working in America and later in England. *Never before has it been suggested that there was this link between the two men.*

Then came the September day in 1950 when Pontecorvo vanished with his family behind the Iron Curtain.

Next to disappear on May 25, 1951—Donald Maclean's birthday—were Maclean and fellow-diplomat Guy Burgess.

Then silence.

And it was not until May 1952 that Mrs. Maclean learned that her husband was alive.

An emissary from behind the Iron Curtain brought her the

DR. PONTECORVO
Old friend of Maclean.

message, and £1,000 was deposited to her credit in a Zurich bank.

"From this moment onwards Melinda's only purpose in life was to locate Donald, correspond with him and bring him back," says the magazine.

"She pursued this goal with perseverance and subtlety that baffled Allied agents.

"She closed her house in England and took up residence in France. Then in October 1952 she moved to Switzerland.

"She was now in constant touch with Soviet agents, who advised her.

"She settled down in Geneva waiting, in a childish hope that she might eventually meet Donald and bring him back to England under a false name.

"Evidence shows that although she was not a Communist she did not condemn her husband's views, but she did not at that time want to go to Russia.

"Meanwhile in Russia Donald had again fallen prey to

PAGE TWO. COL. FIVE.

"DAILY EXPRESS"
London 12-28-53.

Re: Guy Burgess, et al
Espionage

MAR 24 1954
OFFICE OF THE LEGAL ATTACHE
AMERICAN EMBASSY
LONDON, ENGLAND

DELETED COPY SENT C.B. Mac Donald
BY LETTER JUN 22 1976
PER FOIA REQUEST

NOT RECORDED
191 MAR 22 1954

100- 354/183

feb 5

A

485

The riddle of Burgess and Maclean

▶ FROM PAGE ONE

despondency. For almost a year he had been briefing Communists on allied policy and strategy, atomic installations, Air Force strengths, points of Anglo-American friction. But gradually information dwindled to a trickle.

"He wanted to see his wife and children. He told the authorities, 'I could do much better if I had my family around like

Pontecorvo.' The request went through channels and struck a security snag. Mrs. Maclean was an American and a non-Communist to boot. Only a high official could authorise her entry. The decision was postponed.

"Then in August 1953 came the thermo-nuclear explosion on the Aksu River which shook the world.

"Pontecorvo, hero of the hour, was asked in true Oriental fashion to name his wish.

"One of the things closest to his

heart, he said, was the reunion of the Maclean family.

"Thus the drama moved into its final act. Maclean for the first time since 1951 was able to send a long, handwritten letter by special courier to his wife, telling her he wanted her to join him and how it could be done.

"Melinda had to face the gravest decision of her life. She did not hesitate. She agreed to meet a Russian contact at Majorca where they worked out details for her flight."

48

Mr. Tolson
Mr. Boardman
Mr. Nichols
Mr. Belmont
Mr. Glavin
Mr. Harbo
Mr. Rosen
Mr. Tamm
Mr. Tracy
Mr. Mohr
Mr. Winterrowd
Tele. Room
Mr. Holloman
Miss Gandy

BURGESS MYSTERY: IS HE BACK?

Security men work on clue of the bonded notepaper

HOW DID HE GET IT BEHIND CURTAIN ?

Daily Mail Reporters

THE missing diplomat Guy Burgess, who vanished two and a half years ago with his friend Donald Maclean, has written a Christmas letter to his mother, it was disclosed yesterday. And last night security officers considered this question : " Is he back in Britain ? "

There were some grounds for examining that theory on the evidence available.

The letter was in Burgess's writing ; it was on English notepaper not exported to the Iron Curtain ; its typewritten address did not appear to have been tapped out on a Continental machine ; the letter was posted in the S.E.1 district of London on Monday.

Each clue was examined in detail—and considered in the light of American intelligence reports which say that Donald Maclean visited Paris before his wife and family vanished from Geneva last September.

"Daily Mail"
London 12-24-53

Re: GUY BURGESS, ET AL
ESPIONAGE - R

60 MAR 18 1954

OFFICE OF THE LEGAL ATTACHE
AMERICAN EMBASSY
LONDON, ENGLAND

DELETED COPY SENT C.B. MacDonald
BY LETTER JUN 22 1976
PER FOIA REQUEST

NOT RECORDED
191 MAR 16 1954

By midnight the case-book on this latest development in one of the greatest diplomatic mysteries of all time read something like this:

Guy Burgess's letter was addressed to his mother, Mrs. J. R. Bassett, wife of Lieut.-Colonel J. R. Bassett, at Arlington House, Piccadilly.

THE POSTMARK
In dock area

Its postmark—S.E.1—shows it could have been posted by someone arriving at Waterloo Air Station or by anyone off a ship using the wharves near London Bridge or the close-by Surrey Docks.

There is known to be a large traffic in smuggled letters brought in by seamen in ships trading to countries behind the Iron Curtain—particularly Poland.

In the Thames on Monday were three Russian ships—the Lakhta and the Griboiedov, from Leningrad, and the Lermontov, from the Black Sea. All but the Lakhta have now left.

The only British ship in the river on Monday which had recently called at an Iron Curtain port was the 2,000-ton freighter Baltrova. She docked at Hay's Wharf with a cargo of bacon and ham from Gdynia.

But none of her crew was ashore until the next morning—and the last collection from post boxes in the S.E.1 area was at 8 p.m. on Monday.

Because of the Christmas rush, the envelope bore no time stamp—and, again because of the Christmas rush, its exact posting spot cannot be identified.

THE CONTENTS
Date—but no address

The only date on the letter is "November." It bore no address—and there was a notable absence of the copious supply of facts and gossip which was typical of Burgess's writing style.

But the letter did ask that he be remembered affectionately to

THE SIGNATURE

two friends. He did not name them, but merely wrote " . . . you know."

Last night his stepfather, Lieut.-Colonel Bassett, said:

GUY BURGESS
The man who had little to lose
Page TWO

"There is no possible doubt whatsoever that the letter was from him. It contained intimate terms familiar only to his mother and himself.

"He said he was in good health, and he wished his mother a Happy Christmas and New Year."

And from another source came confirmation that the letter was genuine. Mr. Nigel Burgess, an advertising executive and brother of the missing diplomat, said:

"The letter was signed with a variant of Guy's name which he used when writing to my mother. The phraseology is such that it could not have been a forgery. It was a healthy, happy letter, and did not seem to have been written under duress."

THE NOTEPAPER
'None behind Curtain'

The next clue is the notepaper itself. Shortly after it arrived Colonel Bassett told the Foreign Office. Security officers arrived and noted that:

Two of the pages and the envelope bore the "Basildon Bond" brand watermark. The third page was a different type of paper—possibly of foreign origin.

Mr. Harold King, manager of the stationery department of

THE POSTMARK

John Dickinson, Ltd., manufacturers of "Basildon Bond," said last night:

"None of it goes behind the Iron Curtain. We export a little to Sweden, Belgium, France, and to troop canteens and institutions in the British zone of Germany."

So there is another puzzle: How could Burgess have got any of this notepaper in Prague, where he has been rumoured to

Turn to Page 6, Col.

BURGESS RIDDLE —IS HE BACK?

Continued from Page 1

be living? Of course, he may have taken some with him when he left Britain in May 1951.

That, then, is the report on the first communication from Burgess since a telegram was sent to his mother in his name from a post office in the Rue du Louvre in Paris soon after he vanished.

It establishes almost certainly that he is alive and well. But it still leaves many questions unanswered

FIRST: Who posted the letter? If Burgess is not back, it may have been brought in by a friend or agent—or could have even come through in the diplomatic bag of a Communist nation.

SECOND: Where is Burgess living? The letter did not give any hint, or mention any country passed through since he left Southampton by cross-Channel boat on the night of May 25, 1951.

THIRD: Where are Maclean and his family? The letter did not mention them.

FOURTH: What are both men doing? Again, no clue in the letter.

The Foreign Office has reason to believe, however, that both men have since worked under Communist Government sponsorship, and in circumstances of comparative influence and affluence.

FIFTH: Who are Burgess's two friends mentioned, though not named, in the letter?

One may be Mr. Jack Hewit, plump, bespectacled ex-actor with whom Burgess shared a flat in Old Bond-street, W. They had known each other for 14 years.

MORE PAGES
To a mystery

The other friend may be a young American student with whom Burgess had originally planned to cross from Southampton in May 1951.

But Burgess failed to keep an appointment with the student and crossed the Channel with Maclean instead.

SIXTH: Why has Maclean not written? Again, only he can answer that question.

His mother, Lady Maclean, said last night that neither she nor her family had received any communication.

So the Burgess-Maclean mystery adds a few more pages to its case-book, but still remains largely a mystery.

491

Mr. Tolson
Mr. Ladd
Mr. Nichols
Mr. Belmont
Mr. Clegg
Mr. Glavin
Mr. Harbo
Mr. Rosen
Mr. Tracy
Mr. Gearty
Mr. Mohr
Mr. Winterrowd
Tele. Room
Mr. Holloman
Mr. Sizoo
Miss Gandy

(MACLEAN)
LONDON--FOREIGN SECRETARY EDEN SAID IT IS NOW BELIEVED MRS. MELINDA MACLEAN, AMERICAN-BORN WIFE OF MISSING BRITISH DIPLOMAT DONALD D. MACLEAN, CROSSED FROM SWITZERLAND TO AUSTRIA ON THE NIGHT OF SEPT. 11.

IT WAS ON THAT NIGHT THAT MRS. MACLEAN LEFT HER HOME IN GENEVA WITH HER THREE CHILDREN, OSTENSIBLY TO SPEND A WEEK-END NEARBY.

EDEN TOLD A QUESTIONER IN COMMONS THAT BRITISH AGENTS HAD NOT MAINTAINED A WATCH OVER MRS. MACLEAN BEFORE HER DISAPPEARANCE BECAUSE SHE WAS A "FREE AGENT--NO SURVEILLANCE WOULD HAVE BEEN EITHER FEASIBLE OR PROPER."

HE REFUSED TO ANSWER QUESTIONS ABOUT THE DISAPPEARANCE OF MACLEAN AND FELLOW DIPLOMAT GUY BURGESS IN 1951.

10/26--EG1138A

DELETED COPY SENT C.B. MacDonald
BY LETTER JUN 23 1976
PER FOIA REQUEST

100-374183

100-374

NOT RECORDED
191 NOV 4 1953

NOV 5 1953

WASHINGTON CITY NEWS SERVICE

492

Tolson
Ladd
Nichols
Belmont
Clegg
Glavin
Harbo
Rosen
Tracy
Laughlin
Mohr
Winterrowd
Tele. Rm.
Holloman
Gandy

Cases of Vanished MacLeans Ridiculed by Soviet Magazine

MOSCOW, Oct. 3 .—The Soviet weekly magazine New Times said today there are "no grounds" for the theory that missing Melinda MacLean is behind the Iron Curtain.

This was the first Soviet mention of the MacLean case.

Mrs. MacLean is the American-born wife of a missing British diplomat. She disappeared with her three children from her mother's home in Geneva, Switzerland, last month.

Her husband, Donald, of the British Foreign Office's American Department, and a fellow diplomat, Guy Burgess, disappeared from England in June, 1951.

In an article entitled, "Modern Sherlock Holmes in International Arena" the New Times scoffed at Western press theories that Mrs. MacLean's disappearance was staged by the Soviets to decrease United States confidence in British security.

The disappearance "is insignificant in itself and without the slightest connection with the Soviet Union," the magazine said.

"But swindlers of the capitalist press, intelligence services and diplomacy attempted to transform this 'detective case' into an international political event."

The weekly also disclaimed knowledge of the whereabouts of MacLean and Burgess.

The magazine cited a cable it said was received from Henry Lowry, Washington correspondent of the London Daily Express, asking confirmation of a report that MacLean and Burgess were editing the New Times itself.

"This aroused only laughter in our office," the New Times said, "where MacLean and Burgess were known only through hysterical stories in the Western press."

NOT RECORDED
191 OCT 16 1953

100-37418 3

Times-Herald
Wash. Post
Wash. News
Wash. Star
N.Y. Herald Tribune
N.Y. Mirror

DELETED COPY S   C. B. MacDonald
BY LETTER JUN 1976
DIA REQUEST

Date: OCT 4 1953
493

20 OCT 19 1953

CPSIA information can be obtained
at www.ICGtesting.com
Printed in the USA
BVOW03s0844141216
470789BV00011B/148/P